GUILT, ANGER, AND GOD

BY THE AUTHOR

Fear, Love, and Worship
The Rise of Moralism

GUILT, ANGER, AND GOD

The Patterns of Our Discontents

Christopher FitzSimons Allison

MOREHOUSE-BARLOW
78 DANBURY ROAD, WILTON, CT 06897

Copyright © 1972 by Christopher FitzSimons Allison
Library of Congress Catalog Number: 71-163970

Library of Congress Cataloging-in-Publication Data

Allison, C. FitzSimons (Christopher FitzSimons), 1927-
Guilt, anger & God.

Reprint. Originally published: New York: Seabury Press, c1972.
Bibliography: p.
1. Apologetics—20th century. I. Title.
iI. Title: Guilt, anger, and God.
BT1102.A42   1988   239   87-31226

ISBN 0-8192-1420-5

Printed in the United States of America
by
BSC Litho, Harrisburg, PA

―――――――― TO ――――――――

FRANCES ALLISON ALEXANDER,
my sister, and
JAMES RICHARD ALLISON, JR.,
my brother

———————— ACKNOWLEDGMENTS ————————

Grateful acknowledgment is made to the following publishers and literary agents for permission to use copyrighted material from the titles listed:

The American Heritage Publishing Company, Inc.—Rosette Lamont, "Interview with Ionesco" in *Horizon, A Magazine of the Arts*, May 1961. Copyright © 1961 by *Horizon* Magazine.

Atheneum Publishers—Anthony Storr, *Human Aggression*. Copyright © 1968 by Anthony Storr.

Brandt and Brandt, Inc.—Mary Chase, *Harvey*. Copyright 1943, 1944, 1953 by Mary Chase.

Doubleday and Company, Inc.—Theodore Roszak, *The Making of a Counter Culture*. Copyright 1968, 1969 by Theodore Roszak.

Harper and Row, Inc.—Philip Rieff, *The Triumph of the Therapeutic*.

Houghton Mifflin Company—Archibald MacLeish, *J.B.: A Play in Verse*.

The Macmillan Company—*The Collected Poems of William Butler Yeats*. Copyright renewed 1952 and 1961 by Bertha Georgie Yeats.

W. W. Norton & Company, Inc.—Sigmund Freud, *Civilization and Its Discontents* (James Strachey, Trans.). Copyright © 1961 by James Strachey.—Rollo May, Love and Will. Copyright © 1969 by W. W. Norton & Co.—Bertrand Russell, *The Scientific Outlook*. Copyright renewed 1959 by Bertrand Russell.

The Oxford University Press (London)—Walter Russell Bowie, Hymn 522 in *The Hymnal, 1940*.

Random House, Inc.—*The Collected Poetry of W. H. Auden*. Copyright 1944 by W. H. Auden.

Simon and Schuster, Inc.—N. Kazantzakis, *The Last Temptation of Christ*. Copyright © 1960 by Simon and Schuster, Inc.

The Westminster Press—Edward V. Stein, *Guilt: Theory and Therapy*. Copyright 1968 by the Westminster Press.

The Yale University Press—Erich Fromm, *Psychoanalysis and Religion*. Also Nathan A. Scott, Jr., *The Broken Center*.

PREFACE

MY HOPE in writing this book has been to make it one which an intelligent skeptic will read thoughtfully—that is, a person with some aversion to religious language and suspicion of ecclesiastical biases, but also with some hunger for more than "bread alone." I have encountered many of these skeptics within the church as well as outside.

The book, then, attempts to take responsible account of what perceptive non-Christians have said about the modern human condition and what they have offered by way of analysis and solution. And only after that has been done, do I discuss the Gospel and its message to our discontents. But I do not want to equate my understanding of Christianity with Christianity itself, but only to indicate my intention to be faithful to the Christian faith and to invite criticism on that basis.

On many issues, I feel, the questions of the skeptic are closer to the center of Christianity than the affirmations of conventional church people. I believe Christianity has been hurt as much by its friends as by its enemies. The Christian faith is, in its perennial rediscoveries, as much a delightful surprise to Christians as it is to non-Christians. My greatest hope is that this book will be the occasion for such surprises.

Among the many who have helped me with this book
I thank Milton Crum and John Rodgers for their reading
of some parts of the manuscript, and their advice and sug-
gestions. I am especially grateful to Hugh Caldwell for
showing me the passage I have quoted from Bertrand Russell. Ed Camp and Jack Goodwin, with their staffs, represent what good librarians should be, and more. Whatever
the limitations of this book may be, it has nonetheless been
immeasurably improved by the hard work, superb judgment, and sharp tongue of Bertram Cooper, who saved the
reader from many infelicities and confusions that were in
the manuscript before he read it. Virginia Theological
Seminary has made writing the book possible by a sabbat-
ical leave to the author from teaching and committee meet-
ings. I have missed the teaching but am deeply grateful
for the generosity of the Seminary.

CHRISTOPHER FITZSIMONS ALLISON

Alexandria, Virginia
1971

CONTENTS

——————————— *Part Three* ———————————

PARTICIPATING IN THE PROMISE

CONTENTS

PART ONE

The Discontents
of Civilization

one

FOUR CONTEMPORARY PATTERNS

ONCE WHEN I was visiting with a couple who were old friends, we became so engrossed in serious conversation that we ceased to pay any attention to their eleven-month-old child, who was present. At first the infant just sat quietly in his walker; then he suddenly scooted his small vehicle over to the fireplace and began to shake the andirons supporting the logs. Of course, he gained his mother's attention immediately, and she got up from her chair, removed his little hands from the andirons, and said sternly, "No, David. That is a no-no!" She returned to her seat and we continued our conversation. In a few moments he again scooted over to the fireplace, but this time he shook the andirons so vigorously that, before he could be stopped, the logs and ashes rolled out on the light beige carpet.

This time his mother took his hand and punctuated her no-no with two light slaps on his wrist. He was certainly not physically injured by these taps, but his feelings were hurt and he took himself back to his corner and pouted. I watched David as we continued our conversation. Suddenly his countenance changed and his whole face lit up in a confident and determined way as he scooted over to his mother, took her hand in both of his, and bit her!

Wordsworth long ago noted that the child is father of the man, and in the scene just described we can see in microcosm the essential problem of civilization. Any society, no matter how primitive, requires some restraint, some inhibitions, some no-no's. These restraints and frustrations, however, invariably produce feelings of anger, especially toward the agent imposing the restraint. The more complex societies become, the earlier inhibitions must be applied. While yet infants we must learn to share toys and take turns. At Christmas our fingers are peeled off the toy car which belongs to a cousin, and we painfully and tearfully begin to learn about ownership and property. We must wash our face and hands, set the table, not talk with a full mouth, take out the garbage, do our homework, and not "beat up on" little brother. The more civilized we are the earlier the training, the more difficult the homework, and the less acceptable is our aggression and anger. Immediate gratifications must be postponed; desires must be curbed and disciplined. The higher the civilization, the greater are the restraints. At the same time, acceptable opportunities for venting our anger diminish. At forty, whose hand does one bite when his income tax is due?

ANGER

These restrictions, restraints, inhibitions, disciplines, curbs, postponements, and no-no's are part of what is meant

3

by civilization. One of the pervasive discontents of civilization is the anger it triggers and nurtures. This anger is often masked, veiled, and hidden as we grow older, but nevertheless it is there in us all and is a prime cause of our discontent. Unrelieved and mounting anger seems to be the price we must pay for being civilized.

True, there are some release valves in civilization that serve to dissipate our anger. One of them, for example, is blood sport. Anger, which is built up in the process of frustration and restrictions, is released on a scapegoat or, vicariously, in watching bulldogs, bred to fight bulls, being gored and, in turn, tearing the flesh of an enraged animal fighting for his life. Bull fights are another obvious example, but one has to see a cock fight to appreciate fully the frightening violence and aggression released in an arena. I once watched a cock fight, with its blaze of color and the incredibly swift motions of the fighting cocks, bred for generations for just such a purpose, until finally one lay panting, exhausted, and bleeding on the ground. What was far more alarming than the action in the ring, however, were the eyes, faces, and voices of the spectators caught up in the excitement. They ventilated a degree of anger and hatred that no rational observer would have thought could be present in persons sharing our culture. In cultures that permit cockfighting, however, the sport becomes elaborately ritualized and the presence of latent social anger and aggression is veiled by the ceremony and stylized procedures.

Civilizations, however, have gradually tended to abolish blood sports, and the ventilation of anger has been confined to less ferocious sports such as baseball, basketball, and football. Yet I remember watching a college boxing match in 1944 in which one man, with several years experience in the armed services, was matched against a seventeen-year-old boy. There was no question about the outcome; only whether it would be won by a knockout. At the third and last round the younger contestant was up against the ropes and was being brutally pounded. But the brutality in the ring was more than matched by that of the spectators in the stands. The flower of middle-class society—perfumed, cashmere-sweatered, young ladies—were on their feet crying, "Hit him, Roy! Knock him out! Kill him!!"

Colleges have given up boxing as an intercollegiate sport but it still survives on a national level. In 1963, when ten deaths occurred from action in boxing rings, there was some debate in Congress about banning or severely limiting the sport. At the time, to the surprise of many, Margaret Mead defended the sport. This learned anthropologist argued that the problems of masculine identity and of release of aggression in our society are so acute that, as a nation, we needed to have the option of vicarious experiences of pugnacity and aggression.

Historically, of course, most civilizations have turned to war as the means of expending anger. A tribe, city, or nation usually finds new cohesion and unity when expelling its latent, inevitable anger on another group by the righteous, commended, and approved action of killing its enemies. Between wars we usually manage our anger by having well-defined enemies whom we corporately hate as the cause of our misfortunes. I grew up being taught that the Germans were bad; that the Finns were good (because they paid their debts); and that the Russians were bad (because they invaded Finland). Then, when the Germans invaded

Russia, the Russians became at least temporarily good guys as the enemy of our enemy. The Chinese were good and the Japanese were bad. Now, in one lifetime, it is the Japanese who are good, the Chinese bad. The West Germans are now good. Our own ability to destroy has increased so awesomely, our changes of position are so rapid, and the stakes are so high that there seems to be a spreading, semiconscious awareness that we can no longer afford the traditional luxury of hating our enemies.

War is no longer a viable way for civilization to handle its internally generated anger. Civilization controls but does not redeem the aggression it has inevitably nurtured. Our society is now saturated with anger and seems without a safe target for it. We soon learn that an angry person is not successful in business. People will not buy from him. He will not be promoted. He will not be elected to office. He will not become a bishop. A good hostess can "hear" anger at a party and moves immediately to soothe and placate, to change the track of subjects that provoke discomforting feelings. Everyone seems embarrassed and ill at ease in the presence of such anger.

Mary Chase offers one solution in her play *Harvey*, where Elwood Dowd has been taken to a psychiatrist to "cure" him of Harvey (the hallucinated six-foot-tall rabbit). The doctor begins by telling Elwood that if he will only take a cooperative attitude, the battle will be half over, that we all have to face reality sooner or later. To this Elwood replies, "Doctor, I have faced reality for forty years and I have finally won over it. As my mother used to say, 'Elwood, in this life you must be oh, oh, so smart or oh, oh, so pleasant. For years I was smart. Now I am pleasant. I recommend pleasant. You may quote me.' "

6

Civilized society has an awesome need to cover anger with pleasantness. Most of us have learned a little facial trick with our mouths: we have a mechanical smile that we turn on to camouflage the garbage of angry feelings. I once wondered aloud why a certain person seemed always to smile at the most inappropriate times. Someone explained, "He's not smiling, he's baring his teeth!" We smile at the boss whom we would like to strangle. We smile at the customer who is being tyrannically unreasonable. We carry home a load of smiled-over anger, ready to be dumped on any convenient object, and what do we find but a bicycle left in the driveway again. Our son then gets the whole day's load dumped on him.

Statistics concerning brutal beatings of children are so shocking that it seems only social workers are emotionally ready to believe them. Dr. Ray E. Helfer, of the School of Medicine, University of Colorado, states: "More children under five die every year from injuries inflicted by a parent or guardian than from tuberculosis, whooping cough, polio, measles, diabetes, rheumatic fever, and appendicitis combined." (*The Plain Truth*, July 1971, p. 38.) Such savage parental injury to children is not by any means restricted to a particular class or society. The social pressures of public life often push dangerously pent-up anger back into the privacy of the home and put terrible pressures on the family structures when the family itself is least able to bear them.

One more socially acceptable object of anger, one more scapegoat, is left. It is the self. That there is a link between anger and suicide is illustrated by the fact that in England during World War II, when educated, rational, and civilized people of Europe and America were slaughtering each

7

other, the suicide rate dropped to almost nothing. Anger at last had an "acceptably civilized" target. But when victory and peace came, a surprising thing happened—the suicide rate soared! The problem of self-destruction is far more acute in civilized societies than in primitive ones, and, understanding the dynamic of anger, we know why. The outrageous and tragic level of suicide statistics is indeed horrifying, and, let us not forget, the rate is even higher than the records show. Not only are doubtful cases rarely listed as suicide, but many accidents may well have some suicidal factors in them. We often speak of a person drinking himself to death, for example, but it is not listed as suicide. The shocking number of fatal accidents that occur at high levels of intoxication add to the seriousness of the factor of anger in society.

We once lived on a mountain and took turns each week with another family to get eggs from the valley. One morning my wife asked me to pick up the eggs when I was down in the valley. On my return that afternoon she asked if I had got them and I realized that I had not. I started to accuse her of forgetting to ask me to get them, but the ploy of projecting onto her my anger at having to make a second and unnecessary trip down and back was too flimsy even for me. There was nothing to do but accept the blame, and the anger, myself. I got back in the car, consciously and deliberately did not fasten my seat belt, and drove in self-rage down the mountain to get the damned eggs. (A "nice" person does not call them "damned eggs" in his self-rage. A "nice" person swallows all his anger. So many alcoholics and suicides are nice people.)

8

DISESTEEM AND SELF-HATRED

Another characteristic of the civilized person is disesteem, the lack of self-esteem, or even self-hatred. Civilization must not only restrain, it must give ideals, aims, values, goals, and models by which we are to be measured, stretched, and judged. And the higher the ideals, the greater the judgment. We must love our brother, even when he surpasses us at everything. We must not have sex before marriage. We must honor our parents, be unselfish, not have impure thoughts. We must even love our enemies. Under such arduous demands, I look in the mirror and do not like what I see—a walking lie, a hypocrite. If I try to escape this bind by lowering my standards and ideals with such mottoes as, "A dirty mind is a joy forever," then I look in the mirror and see a person with low standards, low ideals, and, of course, low self-esteem. As the inevitable taboos are transgressed, as the no-no's become internalized within us, the conscience gnaws at the heart. When the ideals and standards are not reached but lowered, then the disesteem begins to escalate to the level of self-hatred. And self-hatred is at the root of almost every problem a person faces.

Obviously this lack of self-esteem is related to and becomes an accelerating factor in the dynamics of anger just discussed. Disesteem is fundamental to the whole category of human discontents. If self-esteem is strong enough, anger will be more appropriately handled and the self-damaging aspects of human difficulties will be obviated. Disesteem, however, is the easiest of all personal factors to underesti-

9

mate, and there is no one who does not suffer in some acute way from its pervasive ache. In fact, I am personally convinced that the central theme that runs through almost all the counseling mistakes I have made with people is that I underestimated the disesteem of the counselee. The apparently self-assured are often desperately unhappy with themselves, and the obnoxiously conceited are invariably attempting to cover themselves with an impervious shell that will not disclose this self-hatred. Many very strong personalities with unusual talent, prestige, and power show their gnawing disesteem by their surprising vanity, their constant desire to be flattered, and their persistent need for reassurance. Gaining power does not mean gaining self-esteem.

Disesteem is at the center of all vicious circles of self-defeating, destructive acts. The compulsive gambler, the over-eater, the sexually promiscuous, the procrastinator, the temper-loser, the gossiper, the heavy drinker—all testify to the fact that their temptations are strongest when they like themselves least. From the most serious and extreme to the mildest and most conventional problem, its power over us is in proportion to the weakness of our self-esteem. Succumbing to temptation gives further evidence of and justification for self-dislike. Further loss of self-esteem weakens the strength one has in the face of subsequent temptations which in turn accelerate the process from mild disesteem to flagrant self-hatred. Any help given to child or adult, criminal or patient, parishioner or spouse, must at some point, to be successful, break that vicious circle with something that increases and nurtures self-esteem. Every aspect of the problem of being human and each discontent of civilization is fundamentally related to this dis-ease.

GUILT

In addition to anger and disesteem there is a third acute discontent of civilization: guilt. The essential structures of civilization are meant to inhibit instinctual gratifications, or to encourage the renunciation of them. Such renunciations give rise to a conscience which tends to find further renunciations necessary. In *Civilization and Its Discontents*, Freud admits to his readers his virtual preoccupation with the problem of guilt: ". . . but it faithfully corresponds to my intention to represent the sense of guilt as the most important problem in the evolution of culture, and to convey that the price of progress in civilization is paid in forfeiting happiness through the heightening of the sense of guilt." He then quotes Hamlet to the effect that conscience "doth make cowards of us all."

Much of our present dis-ease is caused by such guilt, but to appreciate its sabotaging power we must understand how large a part of guilt is below the level of consciousness. We are seldom aware of the guilt which is doing us the most serious damage. One of the best treatments of how our unresolved guilt is so destructive of self is Edmund Bergler's *The Principles of Self-Damage*. He shows how guilt has a way of working itself out in us on unconscious levels with self-sabotaging and self-damaging results. A wife will be paralyzed in apparent apathy in the face of her husband's persistent infidelity. When she is confronted with her inaction and inability to protest, she is heard to mumble something like: "I am the last person to have a right to object to someone's sex life." Her unresolved guilt over a long past sexual transgression has left her with a guilt that inhibits her from effectively fighting for her marriage and family.

The politician is often rendered mute and silent in the face of scandal because of his own guilt over some similar question. A college chaplain, who is an old acquaintance, insists that he has known no student to fail merely for academic reasons. "They all had an emotional need to fail. They flunk out because of some deep and usually unconscious need to fail." Incidentally, this phenomenon is quite often related to the sense of guilt which the student has about his relationship with his parents. Unresolved guilt creates a need to make amends, to make restitution, to suffer enough to pay back what is amiss, to set things "right" by damage to self and thus balance the "crime." Psychiatrists and counselors in clinical situations are well aware of the dynamics of masochism, but Bergler has convincingly shown that it is not merely a problem with a few extreme neurotics called masochists (those who gain neurotic pleasure from their own pain), but it is very much a factor in every person.

Many of us feel embarrassed when we are complimented, when people say nice things about us. We find ourselves strangely ill at ease when something wonderful happens to us, as though we did not deserve it. Guilt tends to rob the self of any sense of well-being and does not allow us to enjoy fully our health, wealth, and well-being while we have them. It leads us to expect misfortune, the malfunctioning of machines, hostility from people. And what we expect becomes a factor in evoking what we receive.

More insidious, however, is the guilt which tends to feed our disesteem and self-hatred. One of the most acute symptoms of unresolved guilt is depression. Enormous amounts of psychic energy are expended in what one might call "emotional isometric exercises" that leave a person listless, without energy, and depressed, with only the vaguest feeling of what is wrong. We can push, pull, and press against opposing forces within us and become exhausted without having accomplished anything.

The inability to complete our grief-work over the death of someone close often results in prolonged depression caused by unrecognized and unresolved guilt. We withdraw from friendships, from lively participation in marriage, and from life itself. We do this, in part, because our guilt has injured our sense of deserving and leads us to make restitution by self-damage and the compensation of living less.

DEATH

Freud saw guilt as the greatest enemy of an individual and of a civilization because it is the dynamic behind our self-destruction. The ultimate solution to the problem of guilt is destruction. We resolve our guilt by little deaths of withdrawal from life and by the hope of compensation in self-damaging behavior. It is not just the compulsive gambler, the alcoholic, or the neurotically accident-prone personalities who are the victims of self-damage. All of us to some extent, not only as individuals but as entire nations and cultures, get involved in patterns that are drastically self-damaging and even threaten our very existence.

Some recent statistics have shown that the propaganda encouraging people to stop smoking, which used such weighty and threatening material as likelihood of death by cancer, was not as effective as that which emphasized that smoking would cause bad breath. The threat of death is not as great a deterrent as rational people would expect, because death is precisely what is in part wished for within the guilt-provoked heart of man. Serious studies have shown that the death penalty is not as effective a deterrent to crime as has been traditionally supposed. Many criminals harbor within themselves such patterns of self-damage that punishment by death does not deter them, because death is precisely what the dark side of their character desires. Suicide is one of the major causes of death, especially among adolescents, and there are an infinite variety of lesser suicidal type actions that we all engage in. These are not relieved but accentuated by the pressures of civilization.

Death is thus a major discontent of civilization, not just because of its enhancement by guilt or because of the debilitation ensuing from lowered self-esteem and increased self-hatred, but also because of the anxiety over becoming an ultimate object of dammed-up anger. Death is the discontent that casts the shadow of meaninglessness over all aspects of life. Civilization rests upon the presumed meaningfulness of the order, structure, institutions, and purpose of life's endeavors. Far more than we are likely to recognize, the threat of death paralyzes much of our endeavor and hope.

It is difficult to find a time in history when a people were as seemingly oblivious to the fact of death as we are today. Professor Nathan Scott claims that we have substituted a taboo about death for the Victorian taboo about sex. We usually deal with the subject either not at all or with the sort of macabre humor generally reserved for subjects whose threat we hope to dispel by laughter.

Wife to husband: "John, did you not have a good day on the golf course?"

John: "No, it was terrible! Do you remember the Jack Smith I've played with for fifteen years?"

"Yes, I do. Did something go wrong?"

"It certainly did! He died of a heart attack on the tenth hole."

"Oh! that's dreadful!"

"It certainly was! For the rest of the course it was hit the ball and drag Jack, hit the ball and drag Jack!"

We are so uneasy about the very subject of death that the historic customs of wearing black and assuming a period of mourning make people so uncomfortable that they have largely given them up. A person suffering bereavement often finds that, in addition to living through the adjustment to the tragedy, he is frequently shunned and avoided because he reminds people of what they wish to ignore. A friend once told me that after her child died she was better prepared to face the pain of that tragedy than "to be treated as a pariah."

Our present attitude is a far cry from the medieval greeting *memento mori* (remember death), which was for that culture a pleasant and hopeful greeting. However, a civilization that largely depends upon its own inner resources for hope rightly sees (even though unconsciously) the fact of death as the prime threat to the meaningfulness of all its institutions, rationales, and endeavors. The selfless service which has gone into the making of all great institutions of modern society—medical, educational, legal, and political— and which draws its strength from hope, is in danger of losing its total rationale in the face of death and its threat of meaninglessness. Hence, a culture that has largely abandoned its hope for life after death needs to ignore the very subject; hence, the taboos and macabre humor. Death, the threat of death, and the death wish; sabotaging guilt and the shame that begs self-destruction; disesteem heightened to self-hatred by the ever increasing demands of high ideals and character; and anger, the polluting by-product of the civilization—all are interrelated, inseparable, and feed one another. None is resolved by civilization but is, on the contrary, heightened, exacerbated, and made worse by the unending social controls.

It is no wonder that there is so much revolt against establishments, institutions, authority, and other structures of civilization. We can clearly see this negative reaction to civilization among the younger generation and artists. Both are wrestling desperately with the problem of identity. Increasingly, each is occupied with the primitive concerns, with earthy and instinctual drives, subjects, rhythms, and art forms. Dances are called "Dog" and "Pony." The lyrics of a recently popular song expressed wistful longing for a primitive fecundity lost in the process of civilization: "I'm a disgrace to the aborigine race 'cause my boomerang won't come back."

The current preoccupation with sex and the pervasive level of pornography can, in part, be understood as a desperate attempt to recover vitality and identity and to repudiate the controlling and corrosive restraints of civilization. One of the puzzling questions of our time, "Why are so many of the art forms today so ugly and depressing?", must be seen in the light of the sensitive person's (the artist's) discernment of the unfortunate effects of civilized controls upon the human psyche. Much of modern theatre has been called "Theatre of Cruelty." It exposes and ventilates and, hopefully, purges and provides catharsis to the seething and damaging anger in the culture. The inexpressible anger, scatology, and physical and psychic violence acted and presented on the stage attempt to arouse and give vent to those feelings in us by acting them out as we cannot do in our lives.

Another development in contemporary theatre is the "Theatre of the Absurd." Here the culturally unmentionable threat of meaninglessness is exposed, faced, and confronted. There is little of what one has confidently expected as necessary for a play to be successful in the works of Samuel Beckett, Harold Pinter, Arthur Adamov, and Eugene Ionesco. In the plays of these men there is almost no action, yet the wordy and seemingly absurd dialogue awakens in the spectator the feeling that he is being exposed on the stage both in the shallow absurdity of his conventional life and in his cry for some meaning in life. It is death and the threat of death that continually raise this haunting and paralyzing possibility that life is absurd.

FREUD'S ANALYSIS

In the chapters which follow, we shall be discussing our human predicament in the terms of the four discontents which we have reviewed here—disesteem, guilt, anger, death. To facilitate our discussion it will be helpful first, however, to look briefly at the analytical model of the problem which Freud bequeathed to modern psychology and which has been almost universally useful to widely varying schools of thought because of its clarity and simplicity.

The basic drive of man, according to Freud's theory, is the id—the power and push and energy that a human being has from the time of conception in the womb to fulfill himself, on his own terms, now. It is essential to life itself. If a baby did not suck, he would be almost impossible to nurture. The id encompasses all the instinctual passions to get what is wanted: food, sex, power, property, and self-preservation. The id is down where the animal growls.

It is obvious, however, that this id must be restrained. And the restraining and restricting principle which governs and controls the id is the superego. Even on the most primitive level and at the earliest point of individual development there are superego controls, whether tribal taboos or simply the playpen enclosing an infant. However, as a society becomes more powerful and complex, or as a child grows older, the superego becomes more necessary, subtle, and complicated. From sharing toys and taking turns to the development of character ideals and selfless behavior the process is at work on both individual and social levels. Especially important is the internalizing of the superego ideals in conscience, making it an internal censor to control, inhibit, and restrain the id. The superego is the conscience, a guilt-producing, shame-exacerbating agency. It is indispensable to attaining maturity as well as to becoming civilized.

Between the forces of the id and the pressures of the superego is the ego. Freud gives very little objective definition of ego other than that it is the self or identity between the id and the superego. (Of course, to define more fully the ego is to beg the fundamental question of what a man is.) Hence, when an applicant for a job or a prospective student has a psychological test and it is said that he has a lot of "ego strength" this is no insult, in the old sense of being egotistical, but quite the contrary, it is a highly favorable comment, suggesting that the individual has somehow been able to function between the pressures of superego and id without losing his strength as a person. It means that he can look in the mirror and see himself with both strong drives and a strong conscience, and yet smile and like what he sees. But in most people it is rather more like being in a vise, squeezed inexorably between two implacable forces giving very little room to breathe the air of joy and confidence and creativity. The general relationship may be roughly, but conveniently, diagrammed thus:

Superego or Conscience
Ego or Self/Identity
Id or Nature

Moreover, the relationship and its dynamics is true not only of the individual but of society itself and we can, without significant distortion, translate Freud's model this way:

Superego translated Civilization
Ego translated Society
Id translated Nature

Freud himself used *civilization* as synonymous with cultural superego. Nature is used here as it has been generally used since the end of the seventeenth century—that is, as referring to biological and existential nature; not as Aquinas, Hooker, Coke, and Blackstone used it, as the essential and fulfilled nature of man.

And finally there is this very important observation to be made. Nature and civilization are not forces external to man with which he must contend. They are also internalized aspects of himself, operative forces within him. Thus man is not only a creature of nature responding to its instinctual drives, but also an active agent of civilizing forces with power to look at and within himself, to know that he is to die, and to exercise conscience and will (not necessarily successfully) in deciding what sort of self he will be. Furthermore, this is true not only of individual man, but of social man—that is, it is true also of society. Therefore, it is not only the self but society that is beset and boxed in by the discontents of disesteem, guilt, anger, and death. Diagrammatically, then, we may visualize the human and social situation which we have been discussing in this chapter as a box on each side of which one of the discontents echoes, reflects, and amplifies pressures on the self.

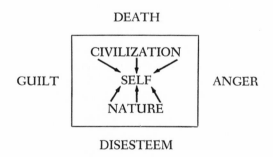

With the help of this diagram, we shall in the chapters that follow undertake to examine the human situation and the problems that result from this complex and dynamic interrelationship. We shall listen carefully to the poignant cry of the artist as he perceives the hurts of modern man and critically examine the suggested solutions to these discontents. We shall only then attempt to see what the Christian faith has to offer to these acute problems of being human, what liberty there is from "The Box."

two

MODELS FOR THEIR RESOLUTION

CONTEMPORARY HOPES of healing our discontents are seen as residing either in civilization or in nature. In the bondage of "the box" man is caught between two rival forces and is forever seeking to mediate between the conflicting demands of culture and instinct. In spite of differing approaches and emphases, modern solutions to the accruing pain of our discontents look either in the direction of civilization or in the direction of nature for easement or relief.

FREUD'S HOPE IN CIVILIZATION

His popular reputation to the contrary, Sigmund Freud argued decisively on the side of civilization. He not only saw clearly the inevitability and desirability of superego development for the individual, but he acknowledged great value in civilization itself. He never suggested that a patient's health could be achieved outside civilization. On the contrary, his whole psychoanalytic assumption was that the patient's awareness of the content of the unconscious and its operative force could give sounder guidance than the irrational forces of the id or the frequently irrational attempts of the superego to deal with the patient's situation. Freud, and Carl Jung even more, were quite definitely on the side of civilization, placing their hopes for man and his problematic condition in a vital culture.

Freud's concept of the id likens it to a seething, agitated stream of energy whence comes man's instinctual power and thrust. Thus, the id, like a turbulent, overflowing stream, needs to be dammed up, restrained, inhibited, channeled, in order to prevent chaos, to harness its power for creative purposes. The restricting and restraining principle which governs and controls the id is the superego.

The necessity for control of instinctual drives by the cultural superego becomes more intense as society grows more complicated and powerful. The ideals, expectations, and obligations of an increasingly sophisticated society demand earlier and ever wider internalizations of conscience and commitment. These, in turn, increase man's disesteem because of the loftier ideals which they set before him, enhance his guilt with broader demands, exacerbate his anger with more frustrating restrictions and fewer acceptable outlets, and yet fail to alleviate the darkening threat of meaninglessness implicit in his death.

In the hazards of negotiating between these conflicts of nature and civilization, the ego or self often gets hurt, mashed, deflated, depressed, even to the point of suicide. First aid is almost invariably a matter of temporarily lifting the civilized inhibitions and superego pressures that are causing this disesteem and guilt, in order to give the ego some breathing room. The immediate relief has sometimes been mistaken for long-range therapy and hence the popular misconception of Freud as an apostle of "letting things loose." Nothing could be further from the truth. He saw the superego development—the internalization of ideals, restraints, and inhibitions—as a necessary part of one's healthy growth into maturity as well as the absolutely essential foundation for civilization itself.

Nature and civilization, then, are not mere external forces with which man must contend. They are also internalized aspects of himself and thus operative within him. For man is not only a part of nature, responding to its instinctual drives, but he is also the conscious subject of civilizing forces with the power to look within himself and to decide what kind of self he will be. Thus man's very condition is problematic: he can look for the resolution of his plight, or at least the easement of his situation, either in the direction of civilization or in the direction of nature. Freud and Jung, as we have already noted, placed their hope in civilization. They are quite clearly cultural conservators, if not very optimistic ones. Karl Marx, on the other hand, was an optimistic advocate of civilization, the inhibiting restrictions of which would soon wither away. He and his followers nevertheless share with western conservatives a hope for the control of nature in some civilized structure.

MARCUSE'S MODIFICATION

Herbert Marcuse, a contemporary neo-Marxian, has had enormous influence on the leadership of the younger generation in the United States and Europe. In his book, *Eros and Civilization,* he has sought to resolve the sinister effect of civilized control on man through the application of Marxian concepts to Freudian theory. In his theory he distinguishes between "basic repression," a necessary and not unhealthy control of man's freedom, and "surplus repression," a gratuitous and unnecessary deprivation that adversely affects the human spirit. Marcuse thus offers the hope of a limited freedom in a limitedly controlled civilization which would make for a little less self-hatred in man, a little less guilt, a little less anger, and a little less fear of death. As Theodore Roszak has phrased it: "This is simply the best we can do." Marcuse's emphasis, then, is on the degree of psychic liberation which must accompany social and political liberation, the whole to be the goal of the coming revolution.

LAWRENCE'S HOPE IN NATURE

But a quite different hope also beckons to contemporary man, one leading him away from civilized controls in the direction of nature. This recent swing toward nature was earlier advocated by D. H. Lawrence, a self-conscious and implacable enemy of Freud. Lawrence saw the mystery, spontaneity, and unself-conscious creativity of man as radically threatened by Freud's teachings, because so self-conscious an approach as Freud's to the instinctual processes of man would intellectualize the genuinely erotic out of life and destroy the possibility of man's achieving innocence or truly creative spontaneity. He declared Freud's system to be simply a new variety of the old Christian moralism, and intellectualizing about sex the functional equivalent of theologizing about God. In Lawrence's view, psychoanalytic theory was destined to give us all a bad case of "sex in the head"—which is not a good place to have it.

Contrary to Freud, Lawrence placed his trust in the irrational, that human element traditionally distrusted by culture, and he saw man's hope for wholeness to lie in the fecundity of forbidden and primitive release. "Blood consciousness," to use his term, would keep man in touch with his vital liberating powers. Modern man, according to Lawrence, is not so much a captive of regimes as he is a prisoner of his own lust for objective reasoning when he should be trusting his own instincts. Hence Lawrence welcomed the imminent end of Western culture and its oppressive and inhibiting institutions; and he detected a sign of this collapse in the modern "scream of violence," that anger which is such a problem for contemporary man. The author of *Lady Chatterley's Lover* scorned the Freudians for destroying the only thing in man that he can trust, his instincts; and he dismissed the Marxists and Socialists for being "preoccupied with the bread question." Knowing that "man does not live by bread alone," he understood the profound and desperate hunger of contemporary man that must be fed on levels of the spirit inaccessible to rationalists and scientists.

D. H. Lawrence's two serious academic endeavors, *Psychoanalysis and the Unconscious* and *Fantasia of the Unconscious,* admittedly were only mildly influential; but it would be difficult to exaggerate the influence of his novels, *Sons and Lovers, Women in Love,* and *Lady Chatterley's Lover,* since today it is the verbal and visual art forms which convey the ideas and philosophy that shape contemporary life. But despite his influence, Lawrence is not so much a shaper of our times as a symbol of the direction so many others have taken in their advocacy of a return to nature.

REICH AND BROWN

In this connection two other influential names should be mentioned: Wilhelm Reich and Norman O. Brown. Along with Lawrence they represent a counter-movement that is as upsetting for Marxists as for the bourgeoisie. In the recent student rebellions in Europe there was not advocacy of one system as against another so much as protest against all structures in the name of instinct and nature. One of the popular slogans was: "A revolution that expects you to sacrifice yourself for it is one of daddy's revolutions." A major influence and authority during these upheavals were the writings of Wilhelm Reich.

The basic theme in the Reichian scheme is that human conflict and sickness are caused by society's repression of the instincts, especially sex. Reich's symbol of man's ills which appeared on the walls of Berlin and Paris (and on American walls, as well) suggests that when the integrated sexual impulse meets repression, the result is conflict between mind and body. Reich believed he had discovered and made accessible the primal energy (orgone) for producing sexual orgasms which in turn cure both emotional and physical illness. His thought was taken far more seriously, especially in intellectual circles, than one would have supposed. He died a tragic death in jail, having been convicted of selling "orgone accumulators" through the mail, a brilliant but sick man. His reputation has now grown to the rank of martyrdom in the eyes of an increasing number of modern Rousseau types who are convinced that the problems of society will be resolved by a return to nature and the repudiation of the repressive and guilt-producing demands of civilization. Lesser followers, such as Lawrence

Lipton, author of *The Erotic Revolution,* are having enormous influence in pop-culture circles, holding out the hope for man's identity and health to be established by a new religion of "pick your orgy," save your marriage by spouse swapping; and by identifying intercourse with deity and blaming all the ills of mankind on the police, parents, the Judaeo-Christian heritage—in short on all restrictions.

Norman O. Brown, however, is by far the most influential among those advocating a return to nature as the direction of man's hope. Like Lawrence, he perceives civilized man's alienation from nature and from his own body. He sees our whole culture diseased by repression at the deepest instinctual level and debilitated by the hidden fear of death. He seeks to restore man to the health, wholeness, and organic unity which predated his repression. Going far beyond Freud and his theory of instincts, Brown plunges into the abyss out of which emerged the visionary worlds of Dionysus, William Blake, Jacob Boehme, and the Christian mystics. Turning the tables on Freud, Marx, and the secular rationalists who were contemptuous of the "fictional illusion" of man-made symbols, Brown maintains that just such imaginative experiences are the "really real and necessary reality" by which nature, man, and man's nature are to be reconciled. "The antimony between mind and body, word and deed, speech and silence, overcome. Everything is only a metaphor; there is only poetry," declares Brown in *Love's Body.*

Lawrence, Reich, and Brown each minimize the political and economic issues and suggest that those problems are merely psychological and/or religious hang-ups that could be resolved by a recovered harmony with nature. On the other hand, they are accused of ignoring or fleeing the real issues of society. Marcuse, as one might expect, insists that what Brown does is to "mystify the possibilities of liberation" and to flee from the "real fight, the political fight."

The influence of the instinctualists is widely apparent in plays, novels, and movies. In *The Graduate* a recent college student comes home to a caricatured parental environment and is manipulated and treated in demeaning ways by the agents of the phony older generation. He is unable to assert himself, apathetic, and without any strength of his own identity and selfhood. After a series of sexual experiences with an older woman, a friend of his parents, his identity crisis is resolved and he becomes a man of action, a take-charge guy who knows who he is, what he wants, and gets it. He is redeemed by sex.

Rachel, Rachel is much the same. Here is an up-tight unmarried school teacher who is pitifully dependent on a neurotic mother and unable to stand up to the principal of the school or to act upon her instinctual compassion for her students. We are asked to believe that after two experiences of sexual intercourse she is transformed into a spontaneous teacher, a strong and compassionate friend, and an independent yet responsible daughter. The portrait of Rachel at the end of the movie is one any psychiatrist could be proud of after three years of intensive therapy. Sex can doubtless be therapeutic, but if copulation is so emotionally hygienic a lot of social workers and professional therapists would be looking for work.

THE CURRENT CULTURAL REVOLUTION

It is easy to ridicule flights into nature without appreciating the compulsive drive away from the squelching influ-

ences of ideals, demands, and constant restraints of civilization that inevitably produce the aching discontents. It is
also easy to underestimate the seductive power which is
implicit in nature.

I happened to be lecturing at a college for women at the
time when John Updike's novel, *Rabbit, Run* was in vogue.
I was astonished to discover that Rabbit, who seemed to me
to be a model of depravity, was regarded by many of the
girls as "real cool" and an attractive figure. On rereading
the novel I noticed that he had indeed "solved" many of the
discontents of being human. He had done this by becoming
an animal. His name was Harry Angstrom and now he was
Rabbit. In the face of any responsibility, he abdicated,
bugged out, ran—*Rabbit, Run*. Hence, as an animal he had
no shame and in running he ducked any responsibility that
could produce guilt. He had "solved" the discontents of disesteem (no shame) and guilt (no responsibility). He
remarked, "If you've got the guts to be yourself, other
people will pay the price."

The contrast of such earthy vitality with the fumbling
hesitancy of the guilt-ridden, over-civilized, jaded young
men these girls often encountered could explain somewhat
their fascination with Rabbit. It also could suggest something of the pull toward primitive or animal models for
identity that we see in such popular movies as *The Fox,
Morgan, Poor Cow,* and *The Virgin and the Gypsy.*

The very subtle difficulty implicit in resolving man's discontents by a return to nature is that, for all the seductive
attractiveness of the theory and the freedom, release, and
remission which it appears to offer, the power gained is
parasitic and temporary. That is, the flight into nature is
romantic and attractive as long as there are other people

tending the store of civilization and providing the structures of efficiency that keep farming and communal living from being a grim, dirty, and unhealthy squabble among still selfish but now primitive individuals.

Equally important is the temporary quality of man's freedom from the laws and restrictions of society. Even Lawrence Lipton's advocacy of freedom in sexual expression has certain limits. "One must not be jealous at a spouse-swapping party." But suppose one is jealous? Then the whole debilitating dynamic of the law enters once again into this new Eden. The more one tries not to be jealous, the more one thinks of it. The more the picture is brought to mind, the more jealous one becomes.

Similarly, freedom from restrictive sexual law becomes bondage to the law of sexual expression. One replaces guilt over being sensuous with guilt over not being sensuous enough; from guilt over adulterous fantasies one moves to guilt over ineptitude or even impotence. The excitement over skinny-dipping is a parasitic excitement which feeds on the cultural restrictions against everyone routinely being naked in front of everyone else. Likewise, much of the admitted power from cultural remissions is a parasitic power which depends for its continued vitality on the inhibiting stuctures of some civilization.

Lowering the level of civilized pressures may indeed ameliorate the intensity of disesteem but it will also lower the level of civilization. Cultural revolution occurs when the tensions reach a breaking point and the remissive symbols are stronger than the controlling ones. Rieff observes: "At the breaking point a culture can no longer maintain itself as an established span of moral demands. Bread and circuses become confused with right and duty.

Spectacle becomes a functional substitute for sacrament. Massive regressions occur, with large sections of the population returning to levels of destructive aggression historically accessible to it."

Although Freud was very definitely on the side of civilization, he was not at all sanguine or hopeful about the discontents being resolved by civilization. He saw that civilization carries the seeds of its own destruction; it produces the guilt which spawns the death wishes which, in turn, undermine its very structure. He ended his book, *Civilization and its Discontents* with this paragraph:

The fateful question of the human species seems to me to be whether and to what extent the cultural process developed in it will succeed in mastering the derangements of communal life caused by the human instinct of aggression and self-destruction. In this connection, perhaps the phase through which we are at this moment passing deserves special interest. Men have brought their powers of subduing the forces of nature to such a pitch that by using them they could now very easily exterminate one another to the last man. They know this—hence arises a great part of their current unrest, their dejection, their mood of apprehension. And now it may be expected that the other of the two "heavenly forces," eternal Eros, will put forth his strength so as to maintain himself alongside of his equally immortal adversary.

In summary we must add that despite science and sex, technology and mysticism, and despite the remissions of many controls, the poignant and wrenching pains of men are with us yet. The cacophony of voices clamoring in contemporary culture—playwrights, artists, sociologists, novelists, therapists, and humanists—are increasingly serious and religious in the sense of attempting to understand and help, to diagnose and heal, to disclose and nurture, to direct and make whole the deep and poignant hurt of being human.

But it would seem apparent from our survey of the models that all the contemporary hopes for solution to the human problem continue to follow, in general direction, the patterns of Freud or Lawrence—toward greater or lesser structures of civilization, or toward nature in the direction either of anarchy and nihilism or of a mystical nature that resolves the conflicts by fleeing them. Thus, disesteem and guilt are resolved by sacrificing man's humanity. Anger and death are overcome by succumbing to them. Man still finds himself caught in the web of his discontents, and the model still reads:

DEATH

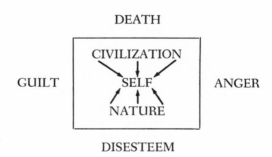

GUILT   ANGER

DISESTEEM

PART TWO

A Different
Promise of Healing

——— three ———
SELF-ESTEEM RESTORED

THE PURPOSE of this chapter is to do something quite simple: to show that Christianity is not a religion of control but a religion of redemption. Or, in terms of the model we have been using, Christianity is not to be equated with superego and civilization but is directed fundamentally to the ego and the self. As simple as this proposition is, the fact remains that many within and without the Christian church have never discovered it. In his book *Freud and Christianity*, Dr. Roy Lee has shown that this was Freud's fundamental mistake, to see the Gospel as superego material.

THE GOOD NEWS LOST

One of the reasons why this simple but fundamentally important foundation of the Christian faith is little known and rarely discovered is that Christianity tends in each epoch to be "domesticated" and acclimated to the contemporary culture, subsumed under the establishment's need for controls, and seduced by the powers of civilization to be its servant. The most obvious illustration is that of Constantine, officially recognizing Christianity first as a legitimate religion and then as a legal one. This latter recognition put the church in the position of being the guardian and custodian of civilization, a position she has largely maintained since that time. This custodial, traditional, controlling responsibility was often urged upon the church by rulers who have always needed religious sanctions for the structure of ethics and justice in a society. Hence, the church was given power, prerogatives, prestige, and a vested interest in the given culture. Of course, these are generalizations and there are many examples of the Christian prophetic spirit being a catalyst and a cause of cultural upheaval, social change, and transition in a civilization. However, the vast preponderance of the Christian role was seen to be, overwhelmingly, that of control rather than redemption.

It is important to appreciate fully the distortion and misrepresentation of the message of Christianity in order to be open to the newness, the power, and the hidden simplicity of the Gospel. One important piece of evidence of the distortion of Christianity as simply superego material is found in the word "preach." This word originally meant the proclamation of the Gospel, of the good news. It has now come to mean, by formal definition: "to exhort in an official or tiresome manner." "Preachy" is defined as: "given to preaching or having a preaching style marked by obvious moralizing." One of the most insulting things that can be said of any art form is that it preaches. I once heard a magnificent lecture by a layman who stated that St. Paul "never preached at people but simply declared what God had done for them in Christ and the consequences of that action for their lives." Of course, this is precisely what preaching was in the New Testament but the lecturer had to reject the word because of its almost exclusive connotation as superego material.

Further evidence for seeing Christianity as only a civilizing endeavor is in the traditional devotional materials written since the middle of the seventeenth century. Sadly typical of this large body of nurturing material are the writings of Bishop Jeremy Taylor (1613–1667). "He that commits any one sin by choice and deliberation is an enemy to God, and is under the dominion of the flesh. In short, he is not a child of God, that knowingly and deliberately chooses anything that God hates." If Christians fail to be like Christ there is no longer any dealing with us by "methods of kindness," and here the wicked hope in vain for pardon . . . because God accepts no breakers of their vows. "[When] the will loves it [lust], and so long as it does, God cannot love the man; for God is the prince of purities, and the Son of God is the king of virgins . . . God can never accept an unholy prayer, and a wicked man can never send forth any other; the waters pass through impure aqueducts and channels of brimstone, and therefore may end in brimstone and fire, but never in forgiveness, and the blessings of an eternal charity."

Christianity was for Jeremy Taylor a promise of pardon, acceptance, and forgiveness *on condition that* the person fulfill the demands of the law. Taylor turned the New Testament upside down: "While we were yet sinners Christ died for us." (Romans 5:8) "Not that we loved God but that he loved us." (I John 4:10) In the New Testament it is the weak, the wicked, the sick, and the sinner for whom Christ died and whom God loves. This message always appears threatening to those responsible for the structures of morality and civilization, and their continual temptation is to turn the Gospel from being good news to the self, pulled as it is between the opposing sides of nature and civilization, to a *promise* of good news *when* the demands of civilization are met.

What is important is not merely the fact that this religion of control was Taylor's presentation of Christianity in the seventeenth century, or that he himself was quite influential (*Holy Living* was in its 14th printing in 1686 and *Holy Dying* in its 21st printing by 1710), but that this mispresentation of Christianity has rarely been criticized since then. (S. T. Coleridge, the poet, is the rare exception.) The uncritical approval of this theology over the past 300 years is important evidence that Christianity has been largely mispresented as only a religion of control and condemnation and that Freud and others cannot altogether be blamed for being led to believe that Christianity is essentially superego material. Theological competence was greater in the seventeenth century when Taylor was known to be Pelagian. A good contemporary definition of Pelagianism would be "nagging."

NOT A GOSPEL OF MORALISM

A religion of nagging—of exhorting and rebuking, of law and control, of condemnation and fussing-at—is a big part of the picture presented as Christianity, not merely by popular distortions but within the very citadels of scholarly learning. The exceedingly influential devotional book *The Whole Duty of Man* sees the Gospel as only law: "The purpose of preaching is to remind us of our duties."

No wonder Sigmund Freud, Erich Fromm, Herbert Marcuse have opted for a more reasonable and less debilitating set of demands and restrictions! No wonder D. H. Lawrence, Wilhelm Reich, and Norman O. Brown flee from such a soul-crushing, esteem-diminishing, and guilt-producing cold system into the arms of the warm fecundity of nature!

CIRCUMCISION AND CIVILIZATION

As surprising as it may sound St. Paul was dealing with much the same mispresentation in his Epistle to the Galatians when he wrote, "Neither circumcision availeth anything nor uncircumcision but faith which worketh by love" (Galatians 5:6); and in the next chapter, "Neither circumcision availeth anything nor uncircumcision but a new creature" (Galatians 6:15). A rough contemporary parallel term for circumcision today would be civilization. Circumcision was for the Jew that which symbolized the covenant with God. The covenant was their law in the broadest sense and the law, the Torah, was the embodiment of their culture, their civilization. Hence, the issue was in large part between those (the pro-circumcision party) who saw Christianity as merely an extension of the old law, and those (the anticircumcision party) who saw it as a complete repudiation of the law itself. It was not unlike "law and order" versus "let it all hang out," or Marcuse versus Brown, or Freud versus Lawrence. In other words St. Paul faced a situation in which some saw the hope for man in civilization; others in uncivilization.

These tensions are still with us today. Many conventional church people and even theologians sincerely see no more to Christianity than the law, the whole body of civilizing and restraining structures and ideals. It is to them what the Law was to the Pharisee. I once called on a lady whose sister had just died. She was not interested in conversing but only sat in her chair mumbling over and over again, "I don't know much about Christianity, but I know the rules, I know the rules." The memory is still a disturbing one. The rules do not give the power to fulfill themselves and a religion of rules *alone* continually undermines self-esteem and erodes what power there is in the self for life and love.

A student once told me about a long bout with a problem he had of "thinking dark thoughts" at Holy Communion. He was a very devout young man and his spiritual director had tried to help him stop this habit for several years. He had a check list of things he was to deal with as preparation for Communion and each time he got to the one about dark thoughts the dark thoughts would return. The rule became the vehicle of the problem. Instead of helping him, it was making matters worse. A system of "help" that required this young man to dwell on the unpleasant symptoms of his alienation was worse than no help and positively harmful. (Such things can be contagious. He even had me thinking during Communion, ". . . now I wonder what sort of dark thoughts . . .")

To understand that a domesticated church tends to lose the essence of the Gospel one must realize that the advice given this young man was representative of "orthodox" moral theology of the past 300 years. The way it prescribed for dealing with intractable and compulsive sins was to concentrate on "elongating the intervals between the commissions." Imagine someone keeping track. "Let's see, last week I went from Monday till Thursday . . . this week it's Wednesday." It's rather like telling someone, "Please don't think of a hippopotamus." Or telling the children in play school, "Now don't any of you put those beans up your nose."

Indeed, Roman Catholicism in the sixteenth century and most of Anglicanism and English-speaking Protestantism in the seventeenth century made a tragic mistake, with sinister pastoral results, by essentially defining sin as being only conscious and deliberate, in spite of the biblical, patristic, and medieval traditions to the contrary. This pushed the root problems of the human heart underground and left the confessional and pulpit dealing with the symptoms of sins, theologically isolated from their deeper, demonic, and often unconscious roots.

The expectation, that a man's will can be changed by exhortations to control, was the essence of Pelagius's heresy, yet it has become a commonplace of traditional and establishment Christianity. There are clergy and church people so emotionally conditioned by this secular world view that they are unable to hear St. Paul's criticism of hope in the law, that system which found hope in fulfilling demands. Sigmund Freud, however, understood the point:

Exactly the same objections can be made against the ethical standards of the cultural superego. It, too, does not trouble enough about the mental constitution of human beings; it enjoins a command and never asks whether or not it is possible for them to obey it. It presumes, on the contrary, that a man's ego is psychologically capable of anything that is required of it —that his ego has unlimited power over his id. This is an error; even in so-called normal people the power of controlling the id cannot be increased beyond certain limits. If one asks more of them, one produces revolt or neurosis in individuals or makes them unhappy. The command to love our neighbors as ourselves is the strongest defence there is against human aggressiveness and it is a superlative example of the unpsychological attitude of the cultural superego. The command is impossible to fulfil; such an enormous inflation of love can only lower its value and not remedy the evil. Civilization pays no heed to all this; it merely prates that the harder it is to obey the more laudable the obedience. The fact remains that anyone who follows such preaching in the present state of civilization only puts himself at a disadvantage beside all those who set it at naught. What an overwhelming obstacle to civilization aggression must be if the defence against it can cause as much misery as aggression itself!

Civilization, like law, is a good thing but it will kill us. This is the paradoxical but simple theme of Christianity. This is why St. Paul can say that the law is "the strength of sin" (I Cor. 15:56) and that it is "holy, just, and good" (Romans 7:12). So civilization for the Christian is holy, just, and good, but it is also the strength of sin. Civilization of itself will not heal the alienation of man.

The nudist and the beatnik, the rioter and the rebel, the anarchist and the nihilist, the free-lover and the pornographer, often discern what many church people have missed —that there is something debilitating to the human spirit about civilization, clothes, laws, conventions, restrictions, governments, ideals, moral demands, and all guilt-producing, conscience-making dynamics. And they are right. However, they are wrong in thinking that their humanity will be healed and made whole by uncivilization, nudity, intercourse, skinny-dipping, orgies, riots, revolution, no laws, or "simple" nature. Neither virginity nor intercourse, censorship nor pornography, reason nor "blood consciousness," submission nor rebellion, police control nor riots, civilization nor uncivilization, can heal man's discontents.

Neither Freud nor Lawrence, Marx nor Reich, Marcuse nor Brown, neither superego nor id, will avail—but a new creature. This rebirth must be in the ego, the self's center, and not merely a recovering of his instinctual nature nor merely control by his rational powers. The proposition can be put:

$$\frac{\text{Civilization}}{\text{Christianity}} = \frac{\text{Law}}{\text{Gospel}}$$

Civilization is to Christianity as the law is to the Gospel. As simple as this is, it is not very helpful unless we understand the Gospel. The law is holy, just, and good but it is the strength of sin. Similarly, civilization is just such a good thing but it also gives power to neuroses, self-damage, ill-health, and tends to repress the human spirit. The question then is: How can we become whole and yet responsive to all the demands put upon us?

SIN DOES NOT MEAN CONDEMNATION

The Gospel is the new condition and it is more than a small presumption to endeavor in half a chapter to provide for the reader the opportunity of being grasped by its power. Yet absolutely everything in the rest of this book must rest upon this foundation: *for one who has heard the Gospel sin does not mean condemnation.* The shock of the Gospel is that it is the opposite of condemnation: the righteousness of God is neither rejection nor condemnation. "For if the ministry of condemnation is glorious, much more does the ministry of righteousness exceed in glory." (II Cor. 3:9)

"There is no condemnation to them that are in Christ Jesus." (Romans 8:1) "If your heart condemns you, God is greater than your heart." (I John 3:20) "For God sent not his Son into the world to condemn the world; but that the world through him might be saved." (John 3:17) In spite of these texts one is scarcely able to use the word sin because it will almost universally evoke a sense of condemnation, largely due to superego Christianity. In order to avoid being misunderstood and because of the almost inevitable inference of condemnation from the word *sin,* I will use inadequate substitutes for the word: immaturity, stupidity, self-damage, self-sabotage, neurosis, infantilism, etc.

Another reason for the contemporary failure to apprehend the Gospel is the threat it seems to pose to civilization. Jesus' great "crime" was his forgiveness of sins and he was denounced by the "righteous" as a friend of sinners and outcasts. St. Paul was repeatedly accused of being an enemy of the law, an antinomian. As the Gospel appeared to be antinomian to the Pharisees in scripture, so it seems anarchic or immoral to those today who would make religion primarily an instrument of civilization.

An even more significant barrier to the apprehension of Christianity, however, is the threat to one's own self-righteousness. The assurance of acceptance, approval, and belonging, as one is, comes only when we realize that we will never achieve this assurance by fulfilling demands. A person who has apparently managed quite well in being "good," observing the rules, and achieving ideals is rich in righteousness, yet it is harder for such a rich man to enter into the kingdom of heaven than for a camel to pass through the eye of a needle. But there is hope for such a man. In the face of the lofty, uncompromising, and absolute demands of the law (e.g., the Sermon on the Mount) he, too, is disclosed as poor, even bankrupt. He now has no self-righteousness to clog his ears from the good news, no frantic hope of super-ego accomplishments to blind his eyes from the vision of the kingdom where he belongs—because he is a son!

In my experience such good people, apparently rich in righteousness, have behind their façade, disesteem of such proportions that they are far from complacently self-righteous. They cling desperately to the little righteousness they do have; they dare not turn loose and relax. They do not hear, not because they are complacent but because they are desperate. The complacent in our contemporary culture are often the outcasts of past cultures. Twentieth century novels have made the prostitute into the heroine. She is the warm, forgiving, understanding, heroic, reconciling "Christ figure." She symbolizes the fact that self-righteousness is perhaps as likely found today in those fleeing culture for nature as in those still desperately hung up on superego pressures.

The difference between superego acceptance and ego acceptance is the difference between being a person on court probation and being a son at home. The former is plagued by suspense without assurance of his future, which is contingent on his achievement. The latter enjoys assurance now, one based not on his *doing* but on his *being,* an assurance grounded on what philosophers call ontology, not on ethics. John Bunyon expressed the self-esteem that is a result of this belonging on the title page of his book, *Justifying Faith*. He had been thrown into prison and ill-used by the civil and ecclesiastical authorities of his day but, with a confidence resting on deeper ground than his own righteousness, he signed his book, "John Bunyon,

Disallowed indeed of men but chosen of God, and precious, I Peter 2:4."

This confidence points to the foundation of the Christian Gospel, unknown to Edward Fowler (Bunyon's bishop) or to Freud. Every other foundation of righteousness—birth, behavior, intelligence, talent, race, wealth, or learning— will inevitably become grounds for pretension and arrogance. There are no ingredients within "the box" that will support the ego. Its support comes from the disclosure of the creating Word.

THE FOUNDATION OF OUR WHOLENESS

Another reason for the present hiddenness of the Gospel message is that the scriptural word *logidzomai,* crucial for understanding this good news, lost its force in English by being weakly translated "impute," a word not often used today. Ever since the sixteenth century other translators have vainly attempted to capture its force with such synonyms as "reckon," "regard as," "account as," or even "think." But none of these words adequately capture the full meaning of *logidzomai,* although it is the clue word to the dynamics whereby a Christian can be responsible to all the valid demands of the superego and civilization without diminishing the power of the id and/or nature, because this Gospel word can also strengthen, empower, and nurture the esteem of man's ego and self. If we can recover this full understanding of *logidzomai,* we shall have gone a long way toward opening ourselves to the experience of the power of the Gospel.

When this word from the vocabulary of everyday, spoken Greek came to be used in the Bible, either in translating the Hebrew Old Testament or in expressing the New Testament message, it took on a personal, a subjective meaning (a meaning, one should add, that it did not previously have in common Greek): such a phrase, for example, "impute to you loyalty" signified not so much that you are loyal, as that I, the speaker, regard you as a loyal person and am responding to you as such; existentially you may or may not be, yet it is in the perspective of your essential loyalty that I take account, regard, treat, and think of you. Thus in scripture we find these sentences: "Blessed is the man unto whom the Lord imputeth not iniquity . . ." (Ps. 32:2) ". . . his faith is counted for righteousness." (Romans 4:5). ". . . God was in Christ reconciling the world unto himself, not imputing their trespasses unto them; and hath committed unto us the word of reconciliation." (II Cor. 5:19).

Now any term that would fully carry the meaning of *logidzomai* would also sum up within it the essence of Christianity itself. But the essence of Christianity can never be a term or a word or anything else short of Jesus Christ. Jesus himself is the meaning of the word, the action, the event by which we are accepted and to be made whole. We can understand this better when we remember that the root of *logidzomai* is *logos,* the word which St. John used in stating the Incarnation: "In the beginning was the Word (*logos*) and the Word was with God and the Word was God . . . all things were made by him and without him was not anything made that was made." (John 1:1–3) *Logos,* then, is the agent of all creation. It is the Word who makes, who creates.

The fundamentally essential affirmation of Christianity, then, is that God was indeed "wording" the world in

Jesus Christ. What sort of God do we have? Before every-thing is the benevolence and kindness we see in Jesus Christ. Who are we? We are the objects of this action; re-garded, imputed, reckoned, treated, thought of, and "worded" not as we are but as we are to be, whole, "chosen of God, and precious." As we have been and are "worded," so shall we be. To be treated and reckoned *as* whole and righteous is to begin to *become* whole and righteous.

Every good parent instinctively knows that a child tends to become as he is treated. A small child may accurately and factually be described as inconsiderate, selfish, self-centered, thoughtless, untidy, undisciplined, and ill-man-nered. However, if he is not seen or regarded by someone as more than that he will have little chance of ever be-coming more than that. Jesus often used the parent-child relationship as an analogy to indicate something of the way God deals with us. ("If a son shall ask bread of any of you that is a father, will he give him a stone?" Luke 11:11) Accurately and factually we are sinners, full of disesteem, guilt, anger, and the fear of death. But God has spoken the Word that "words" us righteous and whole—*logidzomai*.

At the same time it opens up parts of the scripture here-tofore obscured. What in the world does "love thinketh no evil" (I Cor. 13:5) mean? Does this unique love so eloquently described in chapter 13 of Corinthians neither know nor see the evil in this world? Is it some sort of ostrich that fails to face the injustice and innocent suffer-ing in this life? No. Love does not *reckon* evil evil but *reckons* evil good.

Hiam Ginott, the author of *Between Parent and Child,* shows us in very helpful ways the importance of how we go about reckoning children. If a child is bouncing a large ball at six a.m. when you are trying to sleep, you do not say to the child, "You stupid, inconsiderate, numbskull, stop bouncing that ball!" Instead you say, "I am trying to sleep and it makes me very mad that you woke me bouncing the ball!" In the latter case the irritation, anger, and reality is candidly faced but without name-calling the child, wording her character. This fundamental dignity of the child's being, and the value in not disregarding it and bad-wording it, is the core of the wisdom that runs through Ginott's books.

I remember talking with a parent of a boy in the Army who had gotten into considerable trouble. The father asked what I thought of Woodrow. I replied that I thought Woodrow to be a basically honest young man. The father disagreed, saying that he had not trusted his son since he was six years old. Woodrow had denied, even at that age, taking some lead from a plumber who was working on the house. His father had gone into Woodrow's room and found the lead in his closet, where the boy had carefully hidden it in the bottom of his boots. The father said, "That boy has had a bad streak in him from the very beginning." It was as though the father regarded the boy as a product of his wife's bad genes. I asked, "Did it ever occur to you that that is a part of what it means to be a six-year-old— to steal the plumber's lead?" Apparently he never had, and he continued to regard his son as having a bad streak.

There is an apt and profound expression in use among fishermen on the east coast. I remember once getting into a boat when someone said, "I'm afraid we aren't going to catch anything today." He was immediately rebuked by an older fisherman who said, "Man, don't put the bad mouth on this fishing trip!" The father, whom I just mentioned, seemed to be putting "the bad mouth" on his son. You might well ask, "But what if the boy were 16 or 60?" I would reply, "The same thing applies." He must not be bad-mouthed but reckoned or worded as whole. This is not permissiveness nor is it sentimentality. Part of reckoning a person may involve severe punishment, and always involves facing reality responsibly. In fact, part of a person's dignity demands that he be held responsible. However, it does not involve the psychic-homicide of naming and regarding the person as evil.

Every enterprise I know that frees people from hang-ups —from Alcoholics Anonymous to group therapy—is at bottom an attempt to good-word a person, enabling him to accept himself by being accepted and, with this new strength, empowering him to be free of his self-damaging dependence upon alcohol, over-eating, self-pity, or whatever else is sabotaging his humanity. In an experiment in a California school, teachers were told at the beginning of the year that tests indicated certain students in their classes were potential geniuses. These students, however, had been chosen at random with no indication of any superiority. The astonishing thing was that at the year's end they did indeed score far above their previous standing. They had performed that much better than the others because their teachers were tricked into expecting, regarding, and treating them as if they were that capable. "Reckon yourselves as dead unto sin." (Romans 6:11) Because we are reckoned by God as good, we are enabled to reckon ourselves good and this reckoning begins to change us into the good we are to be. With this foundation we are able to reckon others good ("render not evil for evil") and become the means by which others are freed from the prison of their disesteem and self-hatred. Unfortunate and evil conditions are also to be reckoned in this way. In the face of all tragedy we have this good word again: ". . . for I reckon that the sufferings of this present time are not worthy to be compared with the glory which shall be revealed in us." (Romans 8:18) Whatever responsibility we face, whatever there is within us that is tragically not what it should be, whatever evil we think of ourselves, our mutual hope, our common faith and our Christian commitment is that there is no rejection. Rebuke, repentance, responsibility, and restitution, yes; but rejection, no! No matter how evil we may feel that we are, God reckons us good in Jesus Christ. This is what is good about the Good News.

To those outside the church who trust in either civilization or in nature to feed their egos and heal their disesteem, *logidzomai* is an answer to a question they are not asking. To those in the church who trust that what they have done or intend to do will be enough, this news will sound to them as the noise of "drinking and dancing" did to the elder brother in the parable of the Prodigal Son. However, to anyone who finds in himself the abrasive and frustrating effects of repression, of shoulds and oughts, idealism, and control, yet lacks hope of banishing from consciousness such conscience-shaping material by a headlong flight into nature, this is good news indeed. This *logidzomai* of no rejection, this cosmic approval of self, is the aspect of Christianity to which Freud was a stranger. Yet it is the only foundation that will allow us to accept the demands of civilization without sacrificing our nature. It is the foundation of any responsible reconstruction of the Christian message in the context of our contemporary understanding of man and the issues he faces.

four

GUILT REDEEMED

THE AVERAGE person has no more serious enemy than his own guilt. As we have observed in the first chapter, guilt is the crucial dynamic in so much that is self-damaging and self-sabotaging. Freud saw it as the fundamental discontent of civilization, threatening both the culture and the individual with destruction. We can see it in ourselves as the sinister aspect in each of us that limits our creativity, diminishes our self-esteem, enhances our self-hatred. Sometimes it leads us to destructive stratagems of finding scapegoats or to self-damaging attempts to make restitution.

THE INEVITABILITY OF GUILT

Guilt is an inevitable part of civilization. All ideals, standards, rules, oughts, and shoulds of society are pregnant with guilt-making possibilities. In fact, the higher the civilization, the more punitive the superego material; then the greater our guilt becomes both qualitatively and quantitatively. It is not simply the matter of personal sins of commission that create a sense of guilt, but in any politically responsible society there must be a wide and pervasive sense of corporate responsibility. As conscientious citizens we must understand that we are not innocent merely because we were not the direct agent of some culpable act but that we share responsibility if we belong to a society that tortures prisoners, bombs civilians, and pollutes nature. It is not enough to say, "Why, I never tortured anyone! That was Eichman!"

Thus the more responsible the society is, the more complex, broad, and interdependent are the ties binding persons of the society. The moral stability of a given society is dependent upon how much guilt the people can take. Such apparently solid and externally formidable institutions as federal income tax, insurance companies, and the credit system work only because of the intangible willingness of masses of people to judge themselves bound by the moral demands of society. Many cynical things are said concerning the moral state of politics, church, medicine, law, taxes, and education, but the astonishing thing is how relatively well they do work. On higher levels of civilization institutions are built upon ever more exacting demands of duty, efficiency, and morality. This inevitably leads to more guilt. However, when the guilt becomes too painful, the moral demands of the society require the reinforcement of stern external checks and restraints. As the members of society lose their sense of guilt, there must be more policemen and more taxes to pay for the additional restraints, and a vicious circle begins with an increasing loss of efficiency.

We are obviously in a time of such remissive reaction now, and it is important to appreciate the injury and human hurt incurred by the restraining and guilt-producing experience of recent history.

Guilt has sometimes been likened to the brakes on a

car, with the driver as ego, the engine as id, and the superego reflecting the directions and dangers of the world outside the car. Obviously a car with no brakes is a danger
to itself and others. Sociopathic (or psychopathic) persons
seem to have no brakes, to have internalized none of society's restrictions and ideals in the form of guilt; so these
restrictions have often to be provided externally by society
in the form of imprisonment.

On the other hand, however, the opposite is the problem
for most of us neurotics: we are driving the car with our
foot on the brake all the time. We are dragging through
life with our brakes diminishing the power available from
our instinctual nature. This fact is perceived often unconsciously by many in our society as they seek to get in touch
with their feelings through various endeavors that will take
off the brakes that civilization has put on.

Guilt directed inward works against itself; and the tensions between guilt and the libidinous drives can leave a
person in a state of chronic exhaustion with little or no
external mobility. Or the guilt expresses itself in dreams,
and one awakens with no feeling of rest. Guilt also is
often the crucial factor in depression, leaving the self listless and without energy, confidence, or self-esteem, unable
to move or to hope. It takes a certain amount of courage
simply to live at such times. When Freud quotes Hamlet's
observation, "Conscience doth make cowards of us all," he
is pointing to the life destroying dynamic of guilt. It is
no wonder, then, that so many endeavors of society are
attempts to eliminate the guilt that inhibits and threatens
life.

One subterfuge of the superego in dealing with guilt is
to drive a large wedge between our self and our body.

Much guilt is associated with our bodies, and one neurotic way of dealing with such guilt is to dissociate our body from our sense of center. This is one of the decisive dynamics in schizophrenia and it has been suggested that a society can develop a corporate schizophrenia, a split between its rational control and its separated and dissociated nature. Nazi Germany was at the same time the epitome of a rational, disciplined, controlled civilization and a lawless, demonic, chaotic power unleashing unprecedented destructive instinctual force.

It is not enough to say we must keep our instincts under control. Guilt can build up until it is so unbearable that just such a separation can be psychologically inevitable, not just for an individual but for a whole culture.

On another level the widespread growth of group dynamics under an infinite variety of names is an indication of the desperate need for people to get in touch with their feelings and make peace with their bodies. So much of modern art with its primitive themes and "the touch" in what has been called "group grope" is an attempt to be whole again from this split, from this separation from our feelings, and from the alienation of our bodies.

OUR DIVIDED SELVES

T. S. Eliot wrote an essay in the twenties on the work of Milton and Dryden in which he claimed that in the middle of the seventeenth century there occurred a "dissociation of sensibility," a separation of thought and passion. He did not say Milton and Dryden *caused* this, as some of his critics have inferred, but that it occurred in them. He claimed that the blend of thought and passion, so easily accessible to figures of the sixteenth and early seventeenth centuries (Cranmer, Shakespeare, Donne, Herbert, the King James translators), lost that accessibility. Since the middle of the seventeenth century the poet and artist can only rarely and with the greatest agony recapture that association, that blend of thought and passion, reason and feeling.

The demands of civilization always seem to make passion and feeling suspect. They have been driven underground, with only the rarest exceptional person recapturing the blend and wholeness that is the essence of any art form. It was as though society drove away from some picnic in the seventeenth century, having hidden its garbage of passion and feeling with all its organic fecundity. It has, however, a way of calling attention to itself. So after centuries of rational attempts to control passions, of contempt for feelings, and of fear of passion, this whole area calls attention to itself now with a vengeance. With many people it has now become all feeling, all passion, all instincts. Even when the exceptions (and there were many—especially the romantic movements) dealt again with feeling, they almost invariably failed to recapture the old blend, the wholeness of reason and control with feeling and passion.

Because guilt is one of the factors that causes a split deep within us, it must be dealt with if there is to be any wholeness, any health. The attempt to define guilt is rather like the attempt to define light. Everyone recognizes it, but no one is very confident about defining it. Dr. Edward Stein, in *Guilt: Theory and Therapy,* describes guilt in the following way: "It is the dynamic principle operative in man which verifies the fictitiousness of his total autonomy and the validity of his dependence upon all the rest of life, essentially the human community, and supremely, the source and principle of all life, God—the ground of our being."

Dr. Stein's book is one of the rare treatments of guilt, understanding its destructive power but also appreciating its indispensable function as to what is uniquely human. Guilt is that special form of anxiety that reminds us of our essential relationship to others. It warns us against that which threatens life, that regresses to what is inhuman or destructive, and it is a "growing pain" which separates man from beast. False guilt is the twist and distortion of that anxiety which tends to erode our humanity or destroy life.

Many of the contemporary issues in dispute between political parties and the agonizing attempts to bridge the generation gap are related to the different ways people hope to deal with this problem of guilt. Numerous people correctly feel that the essential part of being civilized is to control the instincts, and the chief agent for doing so is guilt. Hence, they look with consternation on all instinctual expression: long hair, discordant expressions of honest feeling, telling it "like it is," casual attitudes toward sexual morality, nudity, using four letter words, and hostility toward police and figures in authority.

On the other hand, there are many whose guilt has incarcerated them from access to their feelings, their bodies, and their very vitality. Radical and painful honesty has become the only instrument that will cut through their bonds; and they are exceedingly contemptuous of conventional and polite niceties they see used to cover and enclose the honest feelings and sources of vitality in the primitive, bodily, and instinctual aspects of man.

A lady, for example, returns from a therapy institute in California feeling like a new person. The pains in her chest are gone. She now speaks with breath coming from her deeper utilization of lungs and diaphragm. She had gone to this institute in a state of wanting to have as little to do with her body as possible. Her speech, posture, and movements all indicated this divorce from her biological nature. By gradual encouragement and reassurance she was reintroduced to her whole self with the help of the authority of the leadership and the support of the group. Touching, honesty, and the recovery of feeling were the means by which she was enabled to break down the wall of guilt that separated her from herself. She had wept and screamed, she had expressed anger and remorse, and had used a vocabulary she did not know she had. But the shame was banished and she felt whole again although the experience violated many civilized and polite things she had been taught.

You can imagine the difficulty she would have in explaining her experience to her mother who had been born on a farm without indoor plumbing, whose sister had died without proper medical care, whose own mother died, worn out and elderly, at the age of thirty-eight. However, the grandfather had managed by heroic discipline and arduous labor to make a good living and she was even sent to college where she met, married, and helped support a medical student. Now, after much discipline and hard work, they have a pleasant and comfortable home with financial security and cultural opportunities—and a daughter who seems to them to be wiping her feet on all the controls, restraints, and disciplines that have guided and structured their lives. The daughter's world, however, is one that understands deeply the sinister effects of guilt on individuals and society.

SPIRITUAL LOBOTOMY NO SOLUTION

Allen Wheelis' book, *The Quest for Identity,* is an important description of that world. His subtitle is: "The Decline of the Super Ego and What Is Happening to American Character As a Result." Our culture is, beyond doubt, beginning to deal with this problem by lowering or even eliminating the superego material that spawns guilt. The positive as well as the negative aspects of conscience-making material of civilization is now eroding. Whether by conscious or unconscious effort, this erosion of the super-ego is an observable actuality, and certainly removes the problem of guilt. However, solution by removal is no better for a society or a culture than it is for an individual.

There are some people who have resolved the problem of guilt in this way, people who resemble Updike's character Rabbit Angstrom. They are often called psychopaths (or sociopaths). They differ from psychotic people in that they have not retreated from the real world nor constructed a psychotic one. They also differ from neurotics in that they are apparently not troubled and pained over their dealings with the real world. They simply do not deal honestly with it and seem to be incapable of feeling any guilt. They are frequently con artists, see very keenly into the foibles of other people, and take unscrupulous advantage in manipulating them. Almost every large office or institution has some story about just such a charming person who hoodwinked everyone and flew away to Brazil with the money.

In telling such stories people usually smile at the charm and trickery, that is, unless they are the victims of such maneuvers or unless the trickster is dating their daughter. However, behind the humor is an exceedingly sad and discouraging situation. Extremely few therapists claim any success at all in treating a full-fledged psychopath, or institutions in rehabilitating one. The prognosis for cure is extremely discouraging. Fortunately, it is a matter of degree for some, and the condition is sometimes combined with more hopeful characteristics that are more tractable to treatment. It is extremely significant that the few therapists who have claimed any small success in dealing with psychopaths (R. Lindner, V. Fox, A. Aichhorn, and Fritz Redl) all seem to depend for success on evoking ultimately some sense of guilt as a necessary handle for help, restoration, reconciliation, and responsibility.

Hence, the solution for guilt by removing it is scarcely any solution at all. To solve this discontent of civilization by removing guilt is to remove one means to man's wholeness. It is to remove a vital organ of his humanity. There was an operation called a "lobotomy" popular in some mental hospitals in the thirties and early forties by which a chronically disturbed patient who was a danger to himself and others, unreachable, obstreperous, and a difficult custodial problem, would have the pre-frontal lobe of his brain severed from the rest. It seems that the conscience and moral censor function of the brain is there, and once that is severed the patient feels no more intense guilt and self-recriminating unrest within himself and he becomes quieter and is easier to deal with in custodial care.

To remove our guilt, even though it is killing us, is like removing a vital organ. When the liver is diseased, doctors do not remove it. It is the only one a person has. Guilt is no kidney or arm, one of which we can do without. It is no appendix that is expendable. As distorted, twisted, or diseased as it might be, it is an essential part of what it means to be human.

What Edward Stein refers to as "the sociopathic drift of our times" is a cultural parallel to the possible schizophrenic state of a whole society. Just as an individual might become psychotic under the tensions of civilization and nature, so a society might become sociopathic (psychopathic) in attempting to resolve the problem of being human by eliminating the superego material.

THE GOSPEL PERSPECTIVE ON GUILT

How then can we deal with guilt? It is killing us but we cannot do without it. Freud saw it as the most important problem in the evolution of culture. Edward Stein says: "Guilt is the peg on which the meaning of 'man' hangs. It is also the peg on which man too often hangs himself." He quotes the British psychoanalyst Ernest Jones, who claims: "The troubles from which the world suffers at present can, in my opinion, very largely be traced to the manifold attempts to deal with the inner sense of guiltiness, and therefore any contribution that will illuminate this particular problem will be of the greatest value." Freud realized that culture is impossible without guilt, and Jones suggests that culture is well nigh impossible with it.

The first step in any reconstruction is to distinguish between neurotic (false) and true guilt. We have enough difficulties already without making friends with false guilt. There is a punitive model of guilt which leads to its being only neurotic or destructive, and there is a reconciling model by which guilt is an avenue to health. As sin does not now mean rejection, so guilt does not now mean condemnation. The last chapter dealt with the grounding and foundation of God's word for us—no rejection and no condemnation. Now the response is one of responsibility. Under God our superego material is loftier, less compromising, and weighted with more relentless demands for righteousness than are to be found in any civilization. "As a man thinketh in his heart so is he." "Be ye perfect even as your heavenly father is perfect." However, the foundation has been poured, we have a place, a home in which we stand, and no law, no neighbor, and no conscience can threaten that home, that Word by which God justified us.

Following Freud's criticism of Christianity, Theodore Reik, in *Myth and Guilt,* insisted that its idealism is too high and that man can only be rescued from this destructively extreme ethic by lowering his ideals. In a society moving in such a direction clarity about oneself supersedes devotion to an ideal as the model of right conduct. The obligation of external ideals is replaced by the obligation to oneself. The harmful effects of the high ideals for most of the psycho-therapeutic world following Freud or Reik obtain only because of ignorance of man's "wording" by God. Justification by faith is as rarely understood by moralists within the church as by secularists outside the church. However, of the two groups the latter are far more knowledgeable and sophisticated about the sinister effects of a religion of law.

The Reformation insight that one's identity (justification) must proceed and become the foundation of wholeness (sanctification) is precisely paralleled by the wisdom of clinical experience of the priority of ego over superego, or the necessity of the self to be nurtured in order to enable a healthy acceptance of responsibility.

Hence the redemption of guilt begins by eliminating the punitive, condemning, and rejecting model of guilt for the human, personal, and reconciling model. Guilt now draws its connotation from the picture of the prodigal son rather than from that of excommunication. Guilt is the human remorse over broken relationships, needless hurt, love unreturned, and goodness violated. It is what Paul Tillich would have called *existential* man, in all his mess, affirming what his *essence* is and tenaciously refusing to confuse his *existence* with his *essence*. The solution to guilt that is sought by lowering ideals and standards and substituting acceptance for forgiveness thereby lowers the hope of man's *essential* nature to the level of his *existential* one. Mere acceptance is forgiveness with man's destiny and freedom amputated.

GUILT AS A WARNING SYSTEM

A helpful analogy is that guilt is to the spiritual life as pain is to physical health. I once read about a boy born with a congenital defect that made him unable to feel pain. My first thought was, "How lucky!" But immediately I knew I was wrong. He had no warning system for dangers to his health. He would not feel the pain of an infected appendix, nor have it removed before the appendix ruptured. If he were fortunate enough to live into his teens he could be talking with his mother in the kitchen with his hand resting on a hot stove and not know it until he smelled his flesh burning. Pain is a sentinel or guard for physical health and warns of possible threats to one's health.

Guilt is like pain in this respect, that the intensity and hurt of guilt is not necessarily an indication of how serious it is. For instance, in the case of kidney stones the pain involved is exceedingly unpleasant yet doctors are very calm and casual as long as there is pain because in spite of the hurt there is really no serious threat to health. However, when it ceases to hurt the doctor begins to become concerned because it could mean that it is not passing and much more serious complications could follow. A hangnail can be more painful than the early stages of some cancers! Some malignant things begin with little or no discomfort and some extremely painful things are no serious threat to one's life.

Similarly, some of our guilt is far more uncomfortable and distressing to us than its seriousness to our spiritual health warrants. I think this is especially true about sex. People almost invariably think "sex" when they hear the word "sin" and yet when St. Paul lists the "works of the flesh" only seven of the seventeen are what we would call carnal matters. (The word "flesh" in the New Testament does not mean "body" and this problem in translation has misled centuries of Christians!) In Dante's *Divine Comedy* the so-called "warm sins" are closer in Purgatory to Paradise, and the "cold sins," are placed closer to Hell.

I remember once walking into a kitchen with a father who was temporarily baby-sitting. His three-year-old boy had been watching television in the basement and had apparently waited too long to go to the bathroom. As we entered the kitchen, the little boy had just lost his race and he was standing in the doorway with his knees together, drenching his pants and weeping with agonizing shame. His father said, "Well, Joe, if you run you can still save some." We both smiled and it was a touching sight. However, it was not in the least "touching" for Joe. He saw nothing to smile about and only the warm accepting humor of his father kept it from being totally and completely painful, shameful, and humiliating. What reader is not touched by this scene and who is so unloving that he does not deeply wish to comfort and reassure Joe that "it's all right and it's not that bad?" "If ye then being evil know how to give good gifts unto your children; how much more shall your heavenly Father give the Holy Spirit to them that ask him?" (Lk. 11:13)

I feel that I must apologize for using such a crude illustration (a feeling prompted by the nurture in superego religion), but that is just the point. Any example of spite or bitterness, vanity or arrogance, self-righteousness or resentment, is far more acceptable by conventional religion yet would be far more spiritually obscene than an illustration of toilet training.

Most of us unnecessarily carry through much of our lives a disproportionate weight of shame for relatively trivial matters. It is quite likely that God looks on such matters with much of the same wistful amusement we experience in picturing Joe wetting himself. The disgrace, disesteem, and shame that we have carried all these years are likely to prove as trivial, in the long run, in God's view as the inevitable accidents incident in a child's toilet training.

Of course, some will say, "But this kid has got to get himself toilet trained!" or "What you (the reader) have done is bad and a sin." Yes, it is important to get the training done as any parent changing and washing diapers

65

knows. However, this is part of being in the parent business. Similarly, part of being in the "God business" is the forgiveness of sins, and there are far more sinister threats to our humanity than the usual things about which people feel so acutely guilty.

Like pain, the feeling of guilt is not an altogether good indication of its seriousness. The intensity of discomfort in some of our guilts is frequently out of proportion to their importance. Similarly, the absence of discomforting feelings of guilt is not necessarily a sign of spiritual health. Looking at life through the closed and dirty window of cynicism rarely is a source of early spiritual hurt. However, like a malignant cancer cynicism can grow until it cuts one off from all love and life. Cynicism, despair, resignation, and hopelessness can begin as wilful defenses, armor against disappointment and hurts. They can grow into such shells that life itself is imprisoned. They are, however, malignant sins and need to be diagnosed and treated early in spite of their failure to produce intense early discomfort of guilt.

Franz Kafka has given us a remarkable illustration of this early and extremely serious guilt that is only vaguely felt. His figure of Joseph K. in *The Trial* has this vague but persistent feeling of guilt but without any awareness of having "done anything wrong." He has been arrested and his trial is coming up but he does not know of any specific charges against himself. Nevertheless his feeling of guilt persists and the only thing to which he can relate it is the fact of his arrest! He seems guilty for having been arrested.

Here the ambiguity of the word "arrested" is pregnant

with meaning. He is arrested but not locked up, not incarcerated. Is he "arrested" in the sense of not growing, not becoming what he is to become? Is his guilt that dim perception of the tragic discrepancy, the painful gap, between what he is and what he is to be? Kafka's character has a way of becoming the reader's own dim and irrational memory of his own dream of himself. Our dreams are often so uneasy that we fail to recall them. However, most of our dreams leave us feeling strangely uneasy, that something is wrong. For Joseph K., representing us all perhaps, it was a guilt over being "arrested," of not growing or becoming what he truly was meant to be.

GUILT AS AN ARRESTED STATE

It is here that the analogy of physical pain must be dropped. This final aspect of guilt is not like pain. With the physical analogy of pain we presume that we come into the world well (with a few exceptions) and that only later we get sick or hurt or out of joint. Physical healing is almost always an attempt to restore one to the previous condition before the sickness. However, in the spiritual realm we come into the world unwell, unfinished, and we look forward to a condition we have not known before.

When we talk about the innocence of children we usually mean by it that their selfishness is appropriate to their age, and they have not yet added to it the subtle layers of adult guilt working itself out in attempts at self-righteousness. Certainly infants do not come into their world thoughtful, considerate, unselfish, disciplined, restrained, and charitable. They do not possess those attri-

butes of love described in the thirteenth chapter of Corinthians. These are attributes into which they are to grow.
As St. Paul tells us, "Eye hath not seen nor ear heard nor
the heart of man conceived of the glory that God hath
prepared for you." (1 Cor. 2:9)

Full spiritual health is not a state of childish innocence
and dependence to which we return, but of adult peni-
tence and freedom we have not known. True guilt will
always render us uneasy with the conditions of ill-health
we resign ourselves to, short of our intended fullness. We
are all guilty over our "arrested" state, and that is the most
important function of our guilt: to push us continuously
from arrested places of sickness to that health we have not
yet known.

One of the saddest people I have ever known was a lady
just back from a clinic. She had felt very bad for months
and her family doctor had finally sent her for a thorough
examination. She had swallowed tubes, drunk barium,
been X-rayed, poked, and stuck for ten days. The final
verdict came: "Mrs. Brown, there is nothing wrong with
you." Her despair was understandable: to feel bad was
her only hope of health; all that she felt was wrong now
was described as the only right she could hope for.

Similarly, to have this guilt, that pulls us to spiritual
health, removed is to leave us in the condition of Mrs.
Brown. The defensiveness and the fear, the loneliness and
lack of love, the sadness and self-hatred now known is all
the health we are to have. No, the very guilt that makes
our dreams so unsettling, that makes us dislike ourselves
as we now are, testifies to a self we have not yet become.
This guilt is a vital organ vigilantly pointing to the discrepancy between what we are and what we are to be.

GUILT AS A REDEEMING AGENT

The secular world, with the best intentions, seeks to remove this guilt from us because it causes such dis-ease and pain. The Christian Gospel is thus a way to word and regard this guilt to make it serve our health and humanity. It is really something to be excited about, something to celebrate. One cannot do justice to such a view of guilt by mere prose. It needs to be done in poetry and sung in a canticle like the one in which St. Francis praised "Sister Death, from whom no man living may escape."

However, I know of no canticle or poem in the history of Christianity which celebrates the Easter view of guilt which we have just discussed. Having no poetic ability, I have found that the employment of an obscure word, a phrase in a foreign language, and a theme from some ancient source will temporarily obscure the absence of talent and set one free to write "poetry."

The word I've chosen is *accidie* or *acedia*. It's so ancient and obscure one may spell it almost any way. Its meaning is akin to sloth or laziness and to anger but it is too angry to be mere laziness, too tired and devoid of energy to be anger. It is a tired and listless anger with no "oomph," or it is resentful and pouting sloth. It is a spiritual malady, especially of dedicated religious people. It is a Lenten or monastic sin. It is a weariness with prayer and with doing good, and has just a dash of rebelliousness in it. It is spiritual apathy. Better, however, than definitions is the picture Dante paints of those in hell guilty of accidie. For Dante, one gets in hell what one wills in life. Those who willed anger, the wrathful, are given back their anger with other angry people up to their armpits in mud, lashing out and clawing each other. The mud is red from the bleeding of scratched and clawed souls, but the people guilty of accidie cannot even be seen. Without the energy of anger they have sunk out of sight into the mud and the only evidence we have of them is the "blup-blup" of bubbles rising to the surface. This is accidie.

I have found a prayer that dates from the fourth century, and was used in a service between Good Friday and Easter since the eleventh century, that provides both the phrase and the theme for the canticle we need. It is: "O happy guilt that merited so good and so great a sacrifice." In Latin it becomes: "O Felix Culpa." Now we have the word (accidie), the language (Latin), and the phrase that is the theme for the canticle (happy guilt). Here is the chance to celebrate the goodness of our guilt, the freedom from losing it and our humanity, and the liberty of living with it happily.

O FELIX CULPA

Praise to thee, dear brother Guilt!
Strong Son of God's law and love
Who dost not cease thy pricks
When we would stoop to play with dangerous toys,
Who goads us from the quicksands of anger and accidie,
Who makes our hearts to hunger
Beyond new clothes, new cars, new kitchens, new houses, new
    spouses, or even a new nation.

I have quarrelled with thee, O Tenacious Shadow that I cannot help but cast as I walk in God's Light.
I have hated thee as the enemy of my sweet sicknesses.

Thy counterfeits have hurt and wounded me.
But thou art the Handle of God's Help,
The Grip of His Grace, and
The Adumbration of My Health;
Thou, in thy True Self,
Art my Glory's True Friend and Brother.
Praise to Thee, O Happy Guilt,
And leave me not 'til we are both at home.

There is no question but that guilt is a shadow in our lives, and a tenacious one. There is a childhood game of trying to escape one's shadow. One attempts to move quickly enough to leave the shadow behind but is unable to do so. Some adults have learned how to beat this game. One can escape the shadow of guilt by going into the darkness. (I do not think it unfair to say this is the poignant and sincere but nevertheless sinister direction of the writings of William Burroughs and other contemporaries who write of sex in almost unrelieved despair as if to find at last some peace at the dark bottom of man's ultimate depravity.) The point to recall is that we would not even know of our shadow guilt if we were not *all* in some measure walking in the Light.

"In the beginning was the Word and the Word was with God and the Word was God . . . and that was the true Light that lighteth *every* man." (John 1:1 and 9) John is not saying that it is the Light that lighteth Americans, or Christians. It is the light that lighteth *every* man. And when we walk in that Light we cast a shadow. To see the shadow of our guilt is just the negative way of saying that the Light is still on! What the world wishes to take away, the Word has worded (*logidzomai*) good.

71

"Let every mouth be stopped and all the world become guilty before God." (Rom. 3:19)

This is not the guilt of rejection or of condemnation. It is now the guilt of sanctification (spiritual health and wholeness) which guards us and presses us on to that health we have yet to know. The discontent of civilization is the guilt by which civilization has come into being and by which its existence is threatened. As individuals and as a culture we can with this redeemed guilt have both a sensuous nature and a sinuous and robust conscience.

Lady Chatterley had her guilt uprooted by the phallic plowing. She said she thought she would have died of shame "but instead shame died." She is symbolic of the reaction against the guilt-producing restrictions of society. Contemporary art forms generally seem to hope for health in fleeing the restrictions of civilization. The second line of defense against the psychically damaging demands of civilization is to concede the demands of personal ethics, thus giving us respite from the implacable superego pressures so we can make a stand on social ethics. Without social ethics certainly no civilization can stand. Hence even the churches seem both mute in demanding individual morality and shrill in exhorting social morality.

Yet the same dynamic applies to social as well as personal ethics and unless we find a way to endure high levels of guilt we will not enjoy a high level of civilization. Professor J. D. Unwin warns us: "Any human society is free to choose either to display great energy or to enjoy sexual freedom; the evidence is that it cannot do both for more than one generation."

This Christian redemption of guilt allows for higher demands than any civilization and without its debilitating effects. This is not merely a good medicine for an individual, it is the only way a civilization itself can survive. Peter Berger has shown us in *The Sacred Canopy* a vivid picture of just how precarious civilization is, hardly more than a small clearing in what is otherwise a jungle. Those who seek to resolve the problem of being human by destroying civilized structures are unaware of how tenuous these structures are. We can get civilization in a somewhat better focus by an illustration of measurement. If we allow an inch to represent a thousand years of man's time on this earth we would have a line 40 to 50 feet long, the last *six inches* of which would represent civilized man. Civilization, although not to be equated with Christianity, is a very precious thing in great danger. Civilization, like the law in Paul's epistles, is "holy, just, and good" in spite of being "the strength of sin." Hence with his guilt redeemed the Christian can love and serve his civilization without believing it to be his hope. God's Word (Christ) has worded (*logidzomai*) us as right, independent of the law (civilization). Now being freed from the law (the crushing power of the superego) we love and serve civilization. This is what it means for the church to be "the servant of the Word to the world."

five

ANGER ATONED

EVEN MORE obvious than guilt, anger is the human discontent which almost everyone recognizes as an explosive threat to the very existence of civilization. The necessary and increasing restraint, restriction, discipline, inhibition, and postponing functions of civilization stoke the furnace of frustration and feed the fires of anger. As we have seen in the first chapter, anger is the immediately discernible result of frustration. Civilization, as the corporate and cultural superego, is a system and structure of frustration and thus an anger-producing process. As civilization grows, so inhibitions and demands come earlier and grow more intense. Children must learn earlier, homework is more arduous, and all professions grow more complicated and specialties more exacting. In spite of all the labor-saving devices, a housewife's life seems more demanding and complicated, and every man's business demands wider knowledge and more preparation.

Our hope has been largely in civilization itself. Christianity, or any other religion, is excused or defended on the grounds that it serves civilization. Many people who consider themselves Christians see its only integrity as a functional aspect of civilization. So often justification for praying, giving, and worshipping is put in terms of helping society. Some of Christianity's warmest defenders have seen it as no more than a service function of civilization itself. Civilization is the real religion of contemporary culture. Part of our present discontent stems from the realization that civilization, that which we ultimately rely upon and put our hope in, is seriously threatened from the inside by anger.

THE NEED TO BE ANGRY

Archibald MacLeish caught the sense of this threat in an article in *The Atlantic Monthly* (February, 1963) entitled "Must We Hate." He showed how civilization seems to breed the sources of its own destruction and, as it becomes more refined, restraints become more numerous, demands weightier, and frustrations more intense. Primitive scapegoats, such as associated with blood sports, lynchings, tribal aggression, and racial hatred, are gradually eliminated or subtly projected to geographically or psychologically more distant objects.

As the process of eliminating the objects of anger, or ritualizing them in sports, becomes increasingly successful we become more aesthetic, polite, restrained, and "civilized." But the anger has not been removed, it has only been bottled up or displaced. As we are taught in physics, matter and energy can be neither created nor destroyed, so anger is still very much with us, in displaced form, when it is merely controlled. Ironically, the need of an object for anger, a scapegoat, is not eliminated but increased by the upward movement of civilization. Anthony Newley's play, *Stop the World—I Want to Get Off*, is in part the artist's cry for us all in our dimly conscious perception of the ride on which civilization is taking us.

We have seen how this need "to get off" is the dynamic behind so much of our present preoccupation with confrontation, nudity, nature, and rebellion against the institutions of civilization. There is much talk of this being a permissive society in reference to the pervasive presence of pornography, the apparent loosening of moral strictures, the appalling rise in stealing, violent crime, and venereal disease. Yet, on the other hand, no society has ever seemed to be so restrained and inhibited by restrictions. Building codes involve not only sewage but style regulations. Schooling, moving, driving, building, buying, selling, taxing, and even dying are far more regulated, involved, restricted, and structured by forms to fill and regulations to observe than ever before in history. In the overall picture it would seem that we are the *least* permissive of any previous society. Perhaps as society eases restrictions in the area of "skin" and personal ethics it is an almost unconscious hope that letting off some of the steam will prevent the pressure cooker from blowing up.

No people were as efficiently civilized, consistently controlled, and industrially "superego'd" as the Germans in the thirties and forties. And yet no people has exploded in such irrational scapegoating as in the systematic extermination of millions of Jews. The anger that is in us as civilized people, however, does not cease to be destructive as we become more primitive, as some romantics suggest. Frustrations under primitive conditions trigger human nature to aggression, as witness Cain killing Abel in the pastoral simplicity of primitive society, a deed as desperate as a murderous mugging in Manhattan. One can be just as dead in a fight over a chicken or a rabbit skin as over land or oil in the Middle East. One does not escape the dangers of aggression by "getting off" in drugs and rebellion against the structures as is shown in such movies as *Easy Rider* and *Alice's Restaurant.*

You may, at this point, be getting the rude and insulting idea that I am saying your anger is working itself out on undeserving and unjust scapegoats as well as eating away at your own vitality as a human—and you are exactly right! However, the problem of being human with a load of anger in our laps cannot be dismissed by attempts to let it loose or by instituting more strenuous control. Both are ultimately vain attempts.

The first step in resolving this acute discontent is the recognition that anger and aggression are not simply the result of frustration. The sources of aggression are deeper than the frustrations of society. Konrad Lorenz, Robert Ardrey, and Anthony Storr have abundantly shown, in the fields of biology, ethology, and psychoanalysis, that there is an instinctual foundation for man's anger and aggression. Anthony Storr, himself a psychoanalyst, feels that his profession is "apt to take too negative a view of aggression and to neglect the more positive aspects." Aggression is a natural and legitimate reaction toward anything that threatens the objects of love. If one is unable to show indignation, it is likely that he cannot show love either. Intense negative feelings toward threats to love are a part of love itself. It is one of the reasons lovers quarrel and families show anger. They do, indeed, love enough to care strongly. There are good aspects of our anger and aggression: it contends against evil; makes no peace with oppression; clears forests, explores new lands (spiritually and physically); pushes through conventional barriers to new truths; defends structures of love; and is indignant toward apathy, cruelty, sloth, needless waste, and innocent suffering.

Hence, it is important that we understand that anger or aggression is not necessarily in itself destructive. Anger is usually condemned in the Bible in some context such as "angry without a cause" (Matt. 5:22) or "let not the sun go down on your anger" (Eph. 4:26). Also, there are numerous illustrations of the angry indignation of Jesus toward the money changers and the Pharisees ("It is better that a millstone be hanged about your neck and you be cast into the sea if ye harm any of the least of these.") Paul is angry with Peter over the latter's attitude toward the Gentiles. He is indignant with the Corinthians as well as with the Judaizers in Galatia. (He even hopes, for those who insist on circumcision, that their knife will slip. Gal. 5:12)

THE POSITIVE SIDE OF ANGER

As our salvation does not destroy our nature, as our ego strength is not gained by elimination of our id, and as our sanctification is not the removal of our guilt, so the Christian solution to our anger does not destroy our aggression. Anger is destructive when it turns to resentment, when it becomes bitter, when it develops into hatred, and when it acts itself out in destructive attacks on scapegoats of others and self. One should no more want his anger treated by its removal than he would want his anxiety removed by lobotomy. Anger is a necessary part of love and of all defenses and protections against death and threatening forces. In addition there is something necessary and healthy in the aggression that is part of all creative endeavors. But as anger produces resentment, bitterness, hatred, and destructive violence it destroys humans and society.

Redemption of anger requires us to face one more, and the most important, source. In addition to the anger that is inflated by social, interpersonal, and civilized restrictions on our natural aggression, there is the anger caused by innocent suffering, the unjust presence of evil, and the heartbreaking tragedies of life. A spastic child is born because of some genetic accident, a young mother of three is dying of cancer, a particularly generous and able doctor is dying of a brain tumor, a dignified and gracious lady is degenerating into a character-reversing senility. To suggest some hidden justice in these matters seems monstrous and insulting to all that we know to be human.

THE OBJECTS OF ANGER

On some adolescent level we can have a rationally angry response to the situation in which a daughter is killed and a mother paralyzed in an accident caused by a drunken driver, who survives with only a bump on his head. We can hate the drunk. But on a deeper, more mature and civilized level we are deeply sad for him and we are bereft of an object for our anger. Even in the case of the brutal murder of six Chicago nurses we question whether the murderer was an earlier victim of some genetic roulette, social irresponsibility, or interpersonal psychic violence. The more educated, perceptive, and sophisticated we are the less we seem able to blame anyone. At least, we are unable to hate them with the older "satisfying" anger of "simpler" times.

But even in "simpler" times men often could not find a

convenient object for their anger at the damned injustice, unfairness, and pain of it all. Men have ventilated their anger in games and sport. Some have retreated in resignation and despair. Some have tried to bury their frustration in the face of suffering by compulsive work or to drown it in drink. But in it all, make no mistake, is anger—cold, hard, and indigestible rage at the unfairness of it all.

I know a church which is an unusually lively place with an unconventional tradition of honestly facing the deep and unpleasant hurts of its people. Therapists send their patients there for the warm and skillful help given in the various parish groups. The clergyman in charge observed with all modesty that he honestly believed they were dealing with interpersonal anger as well as any group in the metropolis but "we don't handle cosmic anger very well." Far more serious than the anger between and among persons is this anger toward God—yes, toward God—a cosmic anger not alleviated by any earthly object.

"Authority problem" has now become a pervasive phrase in our understanding of rebellion. When someone persists in destructive and self-sabotaging patterns of behavior toward such figures as policemen, bosses, deans, and officers it is said that he has an authority problem. "Authority problem" is often thought of as only a problem for young people but there are dimensions of the problem deeper than the relationship with one's father, and the problem persists in everyone in some degree all through life. We gradually shift our anger from those in lower levels of authority as we realize that they, too, are under the frustrations of higher authority. From parents, teachers, and principals it moves to governors, "that mess in Washington," and presidents.

ANGER TOWARD GOD

President Truman had on his desk a sign that became famous: "The Buck Stops Here." Responsibility for difficult decisions tends always to be passed upwards in the chain of command but it always stops somewhere. Decisions have to be made and responsibilities accepted. And yet there is a higher level to which responsibility can be passed. But even Truman or Eisenhower, Kennedy, Johnson, or Nixon can't be blamed for all the frustration, agony, and ills of one's life. The inevitable but unrecognized next step is God.

Anger toward God is said to be one of the strongest taboos in society, so strong in fact that many of its worst victims have disguised it from themselves. But why should we not be angry with God? Is it not his world and is it not imperfect and are we not each cruelly pinched in its imperfections? H. G. Wells paints a portrait of our common outrage. In the muddy trenches of the first World War a young British Tommy cradles in his arms the dead body of his buddy and shakes his fist at the heavens crying, "You blithering idiot!"

Many have replied in vain that it is not God's responsibility but ours. We have misused the freedom he gave us. However true the fact of our freedom is, it does not account for many conditions that no man caused. Of those that man did cause, why do the innocent suffer and why did God not arrange it differently? Archibald MacLeish's play *J. B.* says it simply and unanswerably: "God is God and He is not good. Or, God is Good and He is not God." If he is all powerful he is not good or he would not allow the unjust suffering to happen. If he is good he is certainly not all powerful for his goodness would overcome the evil you and I see.

We must deal with one thing at a time and the point at issue is our anger toward God. We can more often see it first in others. I have spent a great deal of time reading the writings of atheists and I have yet to find one whose fundamental point was not the problem of evil. "Because evil is, God cannot exist." Whether complex or simple, scholarly or journalistic, the atheist's position is saturated with this theme: because of the pervasive injustice and tragic presence of evil God cannot exist.

Our children can teach us a great deal about ourselves. My daughter once came home with the not unusual remark for a nine-year-old, "I'll never speak to Elizabeth again." She was angry with Elizabeth but, either because of the latter's size or the restraining influence of a civilized image of a young lady, she refrained from scratching Elizabeth's eyes. Instead, she did the more civilized thing: she refused to speak.

To act as if another does not exist is a more hostile act than to slap his face. In the latter action one at least acknowledges his presence. The silent treatment is an extremely powerful weapon of aggression. With God, we are seemingly unable to hurt him in any other way. The only weapon we can use on him, as a vehicle for our anger at all the suffering he allows, is our silence. Like my daughter we can at least not speak to him.

Rabbi Richard Rubenstein says that he became a death-of-God theologian the day he visited the extermination camps where God allowed the Nazis to kill millions of Jews. It has become part of the wisdom of pastoral theology to teach that, when confronted with an aggressive atheist,

"seek the source of suffering and try to minister to his hurt."
In the play *J. B.*, the modern Job figure has lost his wealth,
health, and children (the oldest killed through the stupidity
of an officer, the middle two mashed on the concrete high-
way by a drunken driver, and the youngest raped and
murdered by an idiot). Yet J. B. refuses to curse God. "The
Lord gave, and the Lord taketh away" and he is barely able
to choke out the rest, ". . . Blessed . . . be . . . the
. . . name . . . of . . . the . . . Lord." Sarah, his wife,
is furious She refuses to offer the innocence of her children
on the altar of God's goodness and she screams at J. B.,
"Curse God and die!"

At the end of the play J. B. has not cursed God, has not
cursed his only hope for justice; and his wealth, health, and
wife are returned to him. Nichols, the sardonic figure of a
modern Satan, realizes that J. B. is going to take Sarah back
—take her back again and endure all the risk of being hurt
again. He reminds J. B. what she said and did, "She told
you to curse God and die and she left you." And then, in
effect, he screams at J. B., "The only dignity you have left
is your own bitterness—spit in her eye!"

The only dignity we have left is our own bitterness. It
is here that we find the embarrassing truth in God's reply
to Job: "Wilt thou condemn me that thou mayest be righteous?" (Job 40:8) The maintenance of our dignity (Latin:
dignus—of worth), our own righteousness, tempts us to
cling to and treasure our bitterness. The temptation is even
stronger when our cause seems so right. It is ironic that
man's passion for righteousness can be the very occasion of
his anger becoming bitterness. But here God's voice to Job
sets the matter straight. Job is reminded that righteousness
lies with God and not man, that man's self-righteousness is

the cause of anger souring to bitterness. "Beware lest wrath allure thee into mockery." (Job 36:18.)

Anthony Storr's study of the psycho-socio-dynamics of human aggression points out this connection between disesteem (or loss of dignity) and destructive aggression, the perverse tendency to gain dignity through bitterness, hatred, and resentment.

"When a man is, or feels himself to be, an unimportant cog in a very large machine, he is deprived of the chance of aggressive self-affirmation, and of a proper pride and dignity. His sense of ineffectiveness is bound to re-awaken the earliest feelings of helplessness and weakness which he had as a child, with a corresponding tendency for his unexpressed, normal aggression to turn into hate and resentment."

These discontents of civilization can be distinguished but not separated. They are all of a whole. Anger and guilt and disesteem feed each other as aspects of one single unity of alienation, self-destruction, and sin. However, the healing, too, is of one unity, and the weight of anger that pushes toward bitterness, resentment, and hatred is undergirded and countered by the answer to our disesteem, the righteousness by which we are *worded*. That is why any reconstruction must begin with the problem of disesteem and be grounded on the justification that is given by God as we have seen in chapter 3. Those who would have a theology without God (who hope for a solution from within the box) are inevitably back in the quicksand of self-righteousness and ultimately must deal with anger in the inevitably self-destructive and society-destroying ways cursed in the Book of Job.

We all know that Job did not curse God but we often

fail to see why this is so important. He curses the day he was born and he is so bold in expressing his anger toward God that it even frightens Eliphaz, Bildad, and Zophar, his comforters. He contends with God and he ventilates his anger and frustration at the injustice of his suffering. He is anything but patient. However, he does not curse God. Job does not curse his own hope. In all his protestations of innocence his hope is not in his own worth, in his own justice or righteousness. To curse God would be to curse his ultimate, final and only hope that there is justice, a justice beyond his own conception of justice.

Our anger at injustice tempts us to curse God who is our only hope for ultimate justice. This leaves us with no justice but that which we can find in ourselves. The Book of Job leaves us with the hope that rebukes Job's comforters: "For ye have not spoken of me the thing that is right, as my servant Job hath." (Job 42:7) Job's expression of anger toward God is not rebuked but affirmed. Job is rebuked because he speaks without knowledge of the mystery of justice. A third possibility is given:

neither
God is God and He is not good,
nor
God is good and He is not God,
but
God is good and we don't understand.

CHRIST OUR ATONEMENT

However, we have still in our laps this abundant anger and the need to displace it. Is there no more to be said for its resolution than God's "pulling rank" on Job, reminding him (and us) that he is not God and he does not understand? Is it as J. B. asks, "Am I guilty of being weak?" Does this God do more than allow us without condemnation to shout our anger at him and then rebuke us for inadequate understanding?

If we understand that we have a natural aggression which is aggravated by the inevitable frustrations of life, and amplified by the increasing controls of civilization, that we use each other and ourselves as scapegoats, that the deepest aspect of our anger is in the face of innocent suffering and injustice, and that the often unrecognized but primary object of our anger is toward God, then we are at that very center of Christianity asking the question to which the crucifixion of Christ is the answer.

The god of atheists is that aloof and all powerful principle which, because of evil it will not heal, is denied by the atheist in the angry name of his own sense of justice. The God of Christians is he whom we see in Jesus Christ. He takes our resentment in his torn hands, our bitterness in his nailed feet, our hatred in his pierced side and buries them. Yet it is not as a scapegoat that Christ takes our anger but as a lamb. The all important difference between a scapegoat and a lamb is that the Lamb makes us responsible. Scapegoats for our anger are projections that feed our self-righteousness. We always attempt to justify ourselves with scapegoats. The Lamb of God puts the responsibility back in our laps where we are no longer able to justify ourselves because we are held responsible for the death of Christ by our anger toward God.

86

Who was the guilty? Who brought this upon thee?
Alas, my treason, Jesus, hath undone thee.
'Twas I, Lord Jesus, I it was denied thee:
I crucified thee.

This responsibility for the crucifixion is crucial to the experience of Easter. Bishop James Pike once correctly observed that it was necessary for Christians to see themselves as agents of Christ's death to be objects of his forgiveness. Of course, it is obvious that we were not personally there but we are still those people whose anger is only healed by the hurt of Christ. You and I are still the ones for whom it was necessary for Christ to die on the cross for us to live.

Lord, Christ, when first thou cam'st to men
Upon a cross they bound thee,
And mock'd thy saving kingship then
By thorns with which they crowned thee:
And still our wrongs may weave thee now
New thorns to pierce that steady brow,
And robe of sorrow round thee.

To some, the responsibility for Christ's death is no good news. However, building on what we learned in chapter 3 (no condemnation) and in chapter 4 (good guilt), we can realize that being held responsible (able-to-respond) is a new ground and hope for our dignity.

It is strange that the cultural taboo against admitting anger toward God has crept into the church and made us regard it as shocking and something to be suppressed. The thought of expressing our anger toward God in worship is scandalous to many. Yet this is an indication of how far we have departed from scriptural guides. The Psalms, by which Christian people have always worshipped, are generously sprinkled with anger toward God for injustice on earth. Anger is certainly a major theme in the Book of Job. At the very heart of the New Testament men's anger crucifies Christ. Our sickness is our destructive anger. Our medicine is God's taking our anger. If we do not give it to him we are not healed of it. We are in bondage to our anger and are not free until our resentment is buried in him. Yes, as shocking as it sounds, we worship God by expressing our honest anger at him. He can take it much better than our spouses, children, blacks, Jews, police, WASPS, deans, presidents, or ourselves.

The Biblical phrase, "washed . . . in the blood of the Lamb" (Rev. 7:14), which has been so popular with some traditions within Christianity, carries this profound and sophisticated insight: our anger is only here washed clean of resentment, bitterness, and hatred.

six

THE LAST ENEMY OVERCOME

"THE LAST enemy that shall be destroyed is death."
(I Cor. 15:26) "The box" has been broken open on three
sides but the dark fact of death yet hangs over man.

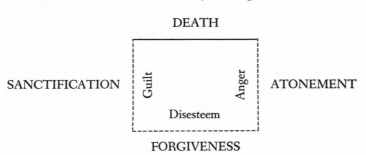

Of all issues the problem of death is the most serious. It
echoes, reflects, and amplifies all of the other human discontents. The shadow of death hangs over all sweat, struggle, striving, patience, love, and sacrifice with the threat
of reducing all to meaninglessness, or to waste.

I remember coming into our kitchen one morning and
finding my small daughter stroking a baby duck lying on

89

the table. The duck was not long for this world; it could barely pick up its head. My daughter was begging the duck not to die: "Don't you die, duck!" "Duck, don't you die!" She looked up as I came in and pleaded with me not to let the duck die. I suggested it might help some if she would stop stroking it but at that very moment the duck had one last convulsion and expired.

She began to cry, not in a whimpering way but with great convulsive sobs. I was quite surprised by this because I had often found children tougher about such matters than adults. After due reflection I surmised that the sobs and grief were not over the duck so much as over death itself. Some time between infancy and childhood we learn on some level about death, and that neither we nor our parents are able to control all things. The apparently all-powerful giantress, who, as Mother, can pick us up, feed us, and make things right, is powerless in the face of death. Dad, who can lift enormous suitcases, fix toys and cars, cannot fix a dying duck. Only one week previously this daughter had seen her father weep at the death of his father. All of a sudden, at six years old, she faced what T. Roethke calls the "immense immeasurable emptiness of things," the ultimate impotence of humans in the face of death.

DEATH IN OUR AGE

Eugene Ionesco relates a very similar incident in his childhood.

I was four years old, and was with my mother in a room. We looked out the window, and there was a burial procession passing by. I asked my mother what it was, and she told me a man had died. Then I asked her how people came to die, and she said that it happened to them when they were old and sick. "And what does it mean to grow old?" I asked. "Does it mean that you hunch over more and more, and that you grow a white beard which gets longer and longer?" Yes, she said, "And does everyone grow old and die?" And she said yes again. Then I started to scream and to cry. I must have cried for hours.

It takes a lot of psychic courage to face the problem of death in any age but today the difficulty is compounded. The tide of the present is against all endeavor to face the issue and has combined with the current of man's natural tendency to escape the problem. Rollo May, in *Love and Will*, writes:

The obsession with sex serves to cover up contemporary man's fear of death. We in the twentieth century have fewer defenses against this universal fear, such as the belief in immortality which armored our ancestors, and we also lack any widely agreed-upon purpose of life. Consequently, the awareness of death is widely repressed in our day. But none of us can fail to be aware at the same time of the tremendous preoccupation with sex: in our humor, our drama, and our economic life, even down to the commercials on television. An obsession drains anxiety from some other area and prevents the person from having to confront something distasteful. What would we have to see if we could cut through our obsession about sex? The clamor of sex all about us drowns out the ever-waiting presence of death.

Our cultural attitude toward death is astonishingly like the Victorian attitude toward sex. We camouflage caskets in much the same way nineteenth-century women dressed to hide their sex. We cover up the dirt around fresh graves with false grass just as the Victorians tried to hide the physical facts of procreation. Death is now unmentionable and embarrassing. It is now the obscene, pornographic subject that casts the awkward silence over social events. In the face of the ultimate impotence that is death's threat we involve ourselves in a compulsive struggle to make ourselves infinite by sex. We attempt to escape the inner dread of death by overcoming it through the symbolic procreation of sexual activity.

Norman O. Brown makes the same point in *Life Against Death*: The great philosopher of organism, Whitehead, has no chapter on death or on the relation between life and death; it seems as if even he bears unconscious witness to the repression of death in the human consciousness."

MODERN SADDUCEES

"The same day came to him the Sadducees, which say that there is no resurrection. . . ." (Matt. 22:23) At the very heart of secularism, the "this-world-is-all-there-is-ism," is the denial of any new life on the other side of death. This belief is so strong that it is almost axiomatic, and just as automatically assumed by modern man as heaven and hell were by medieval man. Even within Christian churches theologians talk of eternal life or resurrection as a *quality* of life here in our time. The author of *Campus Apocalypse* exhorts us to give up any remnant belief or hope in eternal life because it might detract from our commitment to social action here and now in this world. It does not seem to occur to him that giving up eternal life may not enhance a concern for justice in this world but have a different result as St. Paul warned (I Cor. 15–32). It is true that some teachings about eternal life have spoiled endeavors for justice and love in this mortal life, but this is like a man who has been once sick from spoiled meat and turned thereafter vegetarian.

Milton Gatch, for much the same reason, urges us "to continue the tone of the traditional teaching about death [rather] than either its outward form *or its content* [italics mine] because both of these latter conditions are dictated not by the terms of eternal truth but by temporal and cultural and even economic determinants." It is not at all clear why the *tone* is not also dictated by temporal or social and cultural determinants. Nor is it told us what media or access the author has to eternal truth to be so confident that the content of Christian teaching on the resurrection is not of eternal truth. Of course, it might be that he is correct and that the traditional Christian teaching is wrong, but the *only* evidence he has is that *this age* largely does not believe it. Quite possibly this age could be wrong, too. It is a temptation of each age to believe all others are historically conditioned but that this age's beliefs are of eternal truth. The point is, however, that right or wrong the overwhelming belief of the present age is that of the Sadducees who, in our Lord's day, denied the resurrection.

Few today have caught the enormous significance of this non-belief. Hans J. Morgenthau has, in *The Modern Vision of Death*. "It is a distinctive characteristic of our secular age that has replaced the belief in the immortality of the human person with the attempt to assure the immortality of the world he leaves behind." (p. 71) "But nuclear destruction threatens this secular age, which has lost faith in individual immortality in another world and is aware of the impending doom of the world through which it tries to perpetuate itself here and now, is left without a remedy. Once it has become aware of its condition, it must despair. *It is the saving grace of our age that it has not yet become aware of its condition.*" (p. 70)

We are *being made aware* of our condition by modern artists and nowhere so profoundly as in the plays of Ionesco, Beckett, and all those whom Martin Esslin has called the "Theatre of the Absurd." In spite of their "absurdity," they seem to touch a responsive chord in audiences all over modern western culture with their presentation of seemingly irrational, illogical, unconnected chaos, meaninglessness, and despair. One of the most powerful of all these dramas is Ionesco's *Wipe-Out Games,* in which the threat is not so simple and external as mere nuclear destruction but a more nameless, internal, and contagious threat that triggers frantic, destructive reactions of humans in scores of ways. Each scene is a mirror that shows those in the audience their private and sometimes unconscious "wipe-out games" in the face of their own deaths.

"Jesus Christ Superstar," the popular and evocative rock opera, is a reflection of this age's slant on Christianity. It contains six of the seven traditional statements of Christ from the cross but omits, "Verily I say unto thee, today shalt thou be with me in paradise." (Luke 23:43) One of the reasons for study of history is to provide what Reinhold Niebuhr called a "fulcrum of freedom." Every age has its own assumptions and, as children living in that age, we cannot even know what they are unless we, in some measure, get out of that time and view it from the perspective of another time. Only then will we be free to choose which assumptions to maintain, which to question, and which to discard.

We can do this briefly with the early church. The tide of the times was flowing in the opposite direction from that of today. One might generalize by saying that the tide was flowing out of the world through the church into heaven as it has been flowing away from heaven through the church into the world in the past three hundred years. It is a mistake to think of those times as "better." They had their peculiar bondages. Although they found it very easy to believe in God or gods, in immortality and spirit, they generally had great difficulty in believing that Jesus was fully a man, that the body was good, and creation not the source of evil.

Adolph Harnack taught scholars that all heresies were basically either "pneumatic" (spiritual, making religion a flight from creation, body, and the world) or "adoptionist" (Jesus earned sonship by obedience; therefore do so yourselves. Thereby this becomes a religion of self-righteousness.) Perhaps we can gain some leverage on the limitations of our times by seeing in the early church a general (but not total) tendency toward the "pneumatic" or what we might call "bug-out" religion. "The more I see of people, the more I love God." This religion tends to become an escape from duties, responsibilities, and even from life itself. "Pie in the sky by and by when we die" can be (and has been) used to keep people from protesting earthly injustice and to justify cruel oppression.

Robert Frost caught the essential cowardice of this error in religion when he wrote of Christ, ". . . the supreme merit lay in risking spirit in substantiation." It is so easy to be for good things and so hard to put your flesh there. It is not impressively brave for me to tell my wife, "If I were ever to have a baby, I'd do it the natural childbirth way." There is small chance that my opinion will be risked in substantiation. The church had to fight exceedingly hard and even unpleasantly to keep Christianity from being twisted into an easy escapism from a real world, real body, real people, real cross, and real death.

Christians in those early times (with some exceptions, especially in Antioch) had no difficulty with a real God, a real heaven, and a real resurrection. They were not naturalists, materialists, or technologists. Overwhelmingly, they were not what we would call idealists. (So general was their assumption, that their view came to be designated in philosophy by the question-begging name of "realism," indicating the power of a time's tide or the climate of opinion of a given age.)

Today we have little difficulty believing this world is real. We are not apt to blame creation for evil as they tended to do. (There are some exceptions today as there were then.) Many then denied that Jesus was truly a man or that he really suffered on the cross, but they knew he was divine and had ascended into the ultimate and "real" world. Today we seem to have no difficulty believing in a human and very earthy Jesus who did indeed suffer, but we tend to find incredible the hope that "God was in Christ" or that he was raised from the dead.

Simply put, one of the reasons for being a modern Sadducee is that we are modern men. But this may not be as good a thing as secularists are apt to believe. The arch-secularist of the second century was Marcion, who tried to make Christianity into an unearthly, purely spiritual escapism. In this effort he was undeniably "modern." If others had not objected to his eminently *relevant* assumptions in the name of another time, the experience of the Old Testament, we would have none of the good earthy, humanity of Jesus so valued by the relevant, secular, trendy modernist of the twentieth century.

THE PLAUSIBILITY OF RESURRECTION

Let us just tentatively assume the bare possibility that Jesus was right and the Sadducees wrong, that the resurrection might have occurred, and that the injustice in which we all die is not the last word. I am not at this point asking for belief, only for a glance at the possibility of belief.

Amos Wilder explains in part the modern writer's inability to express common grief and love in the face of death on the basis of "sentimental evasion of the incommensurable reality of death." I know of no period in history in which people were so paralyzed and tongue-tied over what to say in the face of death. What does one say on the phone, in a telegram or letter, to a 36-year-old friend whose husband has suddenly died and left her with the responsibility of caring for four small daughters? It is not an isolated, individual, personal matter but a social, corporate, cultural hang-up of these times caused in part by our "evasion of the incommensurable reality of death."

The first step then is to examine our evasion so we may have some control over it rather than vice-versa. It is demonstrably true that in other times the subject of death was not so assiduously evaded nor was it so paralyzing. Unlike previous generations we tend to segregate our older citizens, forcefully retire our experienced leaders, and attempt to cover up every mark or evidence of age. On a personal level many of us have seen in ourselves or others the beginning of confidence and serenity and new life at the very time that death is faced. If we have not seen it ourselves, certainly literature is full of examples of a person's life opening and deepening only when death is faced. It is no accident that the Christian's life begins with death, the death to self in baptism.

Christopher Sutton, in the seventeenth century, had his two marvelous devotional works in the right order. First he wrote *Disce Mori: Learn to Die* and then *Disce Vivere: Learn to Live*. (Jeremy Taylor unfortunately put his backwards: *Holy Living* preceded *Holy Dying*.) We must at the outset swim against the tide of the times and face the fact of death. Franklin Roosevelt had a good measure of theological wisdom in his statement, "We have nothing to fear but fear itself." The fear of death is far more sinister than the fact of death. As I have said elsewhere, in spite of modern medicine, hospitals, doctors, prayer, and spiritual healing the mortality rate is still 100 percent.

The Christian faith claims that, in some way, death as an enemy has been overcome. St. Francis could even write a canticle in praise of "sister death, from whom no man living may escape." One of the things we begin to realize when we confront our mortality is that much of the excitement, tragic heroism, admiration, love, and nobility in people is inexorably connected with the fact of death. Without death there could not be that exquisite aspect of life that is a necessary part of all that is wonderful in humans. This fact is nowhere more apparent than in Greek mythology, where the life of immortal gods is bland and, until mortal man is involved, their story is without a necessary dimension of depth. Sacrifice and pain and love have their price and pulse and power because men do indeed die.

We cannot understand the Christian answer to death

until we withstand the secular pressure to evade it, and much of this pressure has infiltrated the church. However, to be fair to traditional Christianity it must be admitted that any evasion of death is a distortion. "Earth to earth and ashes to ashes" is biblical realism, and the church fought a terrific battle in its early history against those who would not believe that Jesus actually suffered or died on a cross.

Another important but less well known fact about Christianity is the crucial difference between "resurrection of the body" and "immortality of the soul." The latter is not the Hebraic and biblical belief but a part of Greek Platonic thought that had a very large influence on the church as it spread through the Greek-speaking world. Christianity does not have a belief in some separate indestructible part of man called a psyche or soul. There is nothing way down in man that is essentially and innately indestructible, as Socrates thought. Christianity holds to the much more vulnerable but much more total view of man as a whole being. His body, soul, spirit, heart, and mind is one, no part of which can be isolated from the other. In the resurrection of the body the Christian faith holds to the uniqueness, wholeness, and individuality of human personhood. It is obvious that this earthly body decays and becomes meat for worms. Human carcasses dug up are seen to be returning quite rapidly to the dust from which they came. Hence, death represents a far more radical discontinuity in Christianity than in Greek thought. In Greek thought it is but the unseen necessary nature of things that the soul continues after death. In Christianity life after death is far more personal than automatic. It also demands a miracle. "Dust thou art to dust returneth was not spoken of the soul." Here Longfellow is echoing a Greek not a Christian belief.

HINDRANCES TO BELIEF

But the mainstream of modern secularism in contrast to ancient secularism has no such belief in some indestructible soul which will survive death. Modern secularism, therefore, has a vested interest in obscuring the fact of death because it discloses with painful embarrassment the inadequacy of secularism as a solution to the problem of being human. Those for whom Christianity is to be an option must gain some liberty from the bondage of the times that hides from us the actuality of death.

The next step in dealing with the threat of death and the Christian hope of eternal life is a subtle point but most important. Man is a divided animal, he has a mixed and ambivalent will. He both wants and does not want many things. Death is one of them. We have within us some very strong pulls toward death. Some have called them instincts, others wishes, but no matter how they are termed, one of the reasons humans tend to be Sadducees is that they, at least in part, desire death, and not a resurrection. Not only did Jeremy Taylor present Christianity well in his prayers (in contrast to his sermons and other writings) but he also understood most profoundly the "deceitfulness of the human heart." In a prayer he wrote: "I have broken Thy righteous laws . . . was in love with death and dead in sin . . . and loved to have it so." We have seen already, in the actual examples of suicide, how many of us prefer death to life; and we have also seen in the way we live how much subtle and self-damaging death there is in all of us. There is deep ambivalence between life and death in all men and we can so often see in other people how they are their own worst enemies, doing things that damage, weaken, risk, and threaten their lives.

Depth psychiatry has divided this will to death into three aspects: First is the instinct inherited from our biological nature that seeks balance, to come to rest, sleep, death, is called "homeostasis" or the tendency to seek equilibrium. Edward Albee caught something of this tug of death in the midst of life in his play, *A Delicate Balance*. Tobias admits to this shadow over his relationship with his daughter: "If I saw some point to it, I might—if I saw some reason, chance. If I thought I might . . . break through to her, and say, 'Julia . . . ,' but then what would I say? 'Julia . . . ' Then, nothing." Life is always change, adaption, advance, resistance, struggle, and decision. There is something in us that longs to make an unchanging home, to decide nothing more, to give up the struggle, to quit, resign, and drift back into that serene sleep of nothingness. It is called the nirvana principle, the place of no desire, no longing, no growth, no change, no-thing, nothing. Resurrection would upset this and is not desired.

The second aspect, the compulsion to repeat, is akin to the first but an extension of it. We know where we have been but all newness threatens. All strange and unfamiliar things, people, and places tend to make us turn back to known patterns and places. In the face of the strangeness and newness of adolescence, for example, there is the temptation to freeze in infancy. In the face of the responsibility and unfamiliarity of maturity, we tend to cling to our adolescence. In the face of death, we wish for the sleep we have known in life and womb rather than the radical unfamiliarity of a new and eternal life. Resurrection is a greater threat and challenge than adolescence, maturity, or death.

"Primary masochism," the third aspect, is the most difficult to understand by anyone who has not dealt closely with people and who has not had some training and experience in helping them out of binds, blocks, and hangups. However, anyone can look at the history of man and see how he has no enemy as sinister as himself. Those who are so naïve as to think that man's intelligence motivates him would have to submit the judgment that he is stupid to have civil wars, world wars, or even the kind of home-wrecking, heartbreaking, domestic wars in his own kitchens. You and I can say it is "they" or the "enemy" but obviously it is man in the midst of all his heroic and creative genius who continually destroys what he has built and himself with it. History is the history of the rise and fall of civilizations, and the most significant contributing factors in any fall come from within the civilization. This self-damaging principle of masochism in each of us does not want, resists any will or hope for, resurrection.

THE QUESTION OF RIGHTEOUSNESS

The most important barrier to belief in the Christian answer to the question of death is the issue of righteousness. More important than the tide of the times, or this age's tendency to hide from the fact of death, or our ambivalent love of death, or the power of the death wish, is the fact that we do not want righteousness on God's terms. Resurrection means no more and no less than *righteousness on God's terms*. Jesus got himself into that trouble

because his life and teaching judged and transgressed people's understanding of what was right. As we have seen,
man's passion for righteousness is at the same time his
glory and a source of his most insidious sin. The greatest
crimes in history and in homes have been and are perpe-
trated by indignant people in the name of a sincere righteousness. Older ex-idealists, with the burned experience of
cruelty and self-righteousness in the name of good causes,
are tempted to a cynicism that resolves all tension in relinquishing any commitment to what is right.

In a sentimental form this was the deeply disappointing
solution to the play, *J. B.*, after Archibald MacLeish and
Elia Kazan collaborated on the ending for the Broadway
production. J. B. is given back his health, his wealth, and
his wife. Much to Nichol's indignant disgust he takes
Sarah back.

J. B.: Curse God and die, you said to me.
SARAH: Yes. You wanted justice, didn't you?
There isn't any. There's the world . . .
Cry justice and the stars
Will stare until your eyes sting. Weep,
Enormous winds will thrash the water.
Cry in sleep for your lost children,
Snow will fall . . .
           snow will fall . . . .
J. B.: Why did you leave me alone?
SARAH: I loved you.
I couldn't help you any more
You wanted justice and there was none—
Only love.

Here poor, godforsaken J. B.'s hope is only to be warmed
by the love of his spouse "to blow on the coal of the heart"

and to see his cry for justice as his error. To relinquish the hope for justice is to curse God. The reason, as we have seen, for not cursing God is that it would mean to curse one's only hope for a justice in and on the other side of this tragedy, this life, and each man's death.

To trade justice for "love" is impressive rhetoric and clever verbiage but it leaves us with distorted, inadequate "loves." Because of moralism, the words "justice" and "righteousness" too often carry only negative and judgmental meanings. On the other hand, when not being moralistic the ecclesiastical institution has been overwhelmingly sentimental. Part of our modern skepticism concerning resurrection is a reaction to such sentimental misrepresentations of Christianity.

The poet Wallace Stevens objected vigorously to this sentimental "it's-all-gonna-be-all-right" notion. In his "Esthetique du Mal" he reflects on the easy answers that have been given to evil and death and calls out for a "savage honesty" to cleanse man of his fear. The "savage honesty" necessary to make the Christian teaching of resurrection accessible to us has as its target human sin.

"The sting of death is sin." (I Cor. 15:56) A clergyman friend of mine asked me recently in a most condescending tone, "Are you still talking about sin?" I replied that I had searched in vain for a synonym which was not superficial and asked if he had come up with one? He had not. The overwhelming factor in our disbelief in the resurrection is our sin, because resurrection means judgment.

THE STING OF DEATH

There is no way around the tenaciously persistent biblical fact that the God Christians worship is the God of

Righteousness. (". . . this is his name, the Lord our righteousness. Jer. 23:6) It is true, as we have seen in chapter
3, that God declares his righteousness by the forgiveness
of sins and by reckoning (or wording) us as righteous. This
is his way of beginning to make us righteous. We were
squeezed into this world through a narrow aperture and
we shall be squeezed out through a narrow door of death.
The sting of death is sin: sin does not get through the
door, sin is not raised up. Sin will know no resurrection.
That may be harmless-sounding religious language, but let
us stop to think what it means. The racist's fear of and
hostility for blacks (or whites or browns or Jews) will not
come through. It is scraped off. Our desire for revenge
and retribution for those who have wronged us gets jerked
out of our already tender hearts. Our horribly naked
thoughtlessness is glaringly exposed.

For I was an hungred, and ye gave me no meat: I was thirsty,
and ye gave me no drink: I was a stranger, and ye took me not
in: naked, and ye clothed me not: sick, and in prison, and ye
visited me not. Then shall they also answer him, saying, Lord,
when saw we thee an hungred, or athirst, or a stranger, or
naked, or sick, or in prison, and did not minister unto thee?
Then shall he answer them, saying, Verily I say unto you, Inasmuch as ye did it not to one of the least of these, ye did it not
to me. (Matt. 25:42–45)

There is a story about B. H. Streeter, the great New
Testament scholar, who had been passionately involved in
this life with the question of whether or not Acts 15 and
Galatians 2 represented the same trip of Paul to Jerusalem.
When he got to heaven the first thing he did was to seek
out St. Paul and ask him. Paul stroked his beard, thought,
and replied, "I just can't remember." There is every likeli-

hood that many of the issues and crusades we so passionately fight here will be irrelevant or wrong there. Now
you and I will be able to take that quite well but think
how painful this will be for other people! In fact, it is
somewhat clearer to us how painful the just judgment in
the resurrection will be for other people than for ourselves.

I am sure we each know someone who much of his life
has regarded his spouse as a mistake he made but feels he
has gallantly and even heroically endured. Because of his
good grace and spirit there has even been some small
measure of joy and light in his marriage. He believes this
quite deeply and genuinely, with some reason; or at least
we can understand something of how and why he feels
this way. Yet we also know that it is only half the truth
and that his wife, with equal time, could have as much
justice on her side. What would it be like for us to tell
him just exactly how we see the other side? It might well
be the end of the friendship, but if he could "hear" this
through the barrier of hostility he would throw up, it
would cause him far more pain and hurt than slapping his
face. We have all known such people whom we, perhaps
rightly, would not dare confront with what seems to be
the real picture underneath all the self-pity and self-justifi-
cation.

A friend who was in his first year of a full psychoanalysis
told me what the process was like. He said it was like
walking through the world with water up to his chest and
it took all his energy just to walk and not stumble. So great
was the energy required to face the painful reality about
himself, and deliberately encounter what he had covered
up or run away from all his life, that it was exhausting
just to move.

If it is so painful to be healed in this life, we have good reason to believe that in the resurrection it will be no Sunday School picnic to peel the sin off our hides. It will be like jerking adhesive tape off a hairy man. Of course, I don't mean this to apply to the reader or myself, but I am sure we both know others for whom justice will be a painful experience!

Jesus said, "It is easier for a camel to go through the eye of a needle than for a rich man to enter into the kingdom of God." (Matt. 19:24) This is no reassurance for poor people because his disciples immediately asked him "Who then can be saved?" And he replied, "With men this is impossible; but with God all things are possible." (Matt. 19:26) This gate to the kingdom of heaven is a narrow gate that is impossible for man to get through. With the "impossible possibility" of God's action in Christ on the cross and an empty tomb, now the sting of death, which is sin, is removed and the gate to the kingdom is open for us—but not for our sin. That gets scraped, peeled, pulled, removed coming through and we are made naked, divorced, and bereft of our treasured sin. Only we alone, healed and whole, are raised.

One seventeenth-century theologian likened our desire for judgment to our desire "to be cut of the stone." He was referring to the then current prevalence of kidney stones, and considering the quality of seventeenth-century medical instruments a person's desire to be cut of the stone must have been ambivalent to say the least. Our self-pity, self-righteousness, bitterness, apathy and all other sins have become so much an apparent but false part of us, that as we will *them*, we will not will, hope for, believe in, nor want the resurrection. To put it quite simply, inasmuch as we are sinners (and none of us is all sinner) we do not want nor wish the resurrection, righteousness on God's terms.

We must overcome the following barriers if we are to appropriate the Christian medicine for the malady of death: the tide of the times that lures us to hide and ignore death; the instinctual pull toward death; the ambivalent will for death; the psychologically neurotic temptation to freeze in or return to familiar states; the self-damaging masochism in each of us; the weary temptation to resign, quit, and seek nirvana—a nothing state; and, most of all, our own sin, which turns our wills from any hope that threatens our self-righteousness.

One further difficulty is that Christianity affirms no smooth, necessary, and inevitable transition from life through death to immortality as did the ancient Greeks. For Christians eternal life is impossible. As Jesus said about the camel and the eye of the needle "with man it is impossible" to enter the kingdom of heaven. Here is that "savage honesty" needed to cleanse us of our fear of death and our neurotic dislike for resurrection. W. H. Auden has written the cry for any man disabused of his false hopes and dissatisfied with his despair:

> We who must die demand a miracle.
> How could the Eternal do a temporal act,
> The Infinite become a finite fact?
> Nothing can save us that is possible:
> We who must die demand a miracle.
>
> From W. H. Auden's "For the Time Being"

"With men this is impossible; but with God all things are possible." This is what Reinhold Niebuhr called the "impossible possibility" and the Christian faith is that it has been done. This faith does the following things: It gives us hope, from which comes the power to face death. In facing death this dimension of eternal life begins now. Karl Barth tells us that "life emerges at the point of mortification" and Kierkegaard says that "the inevitability of death accepted at the highest level of passion is an empowering thing." To avoid sentimental and shallow distortions of Christianity, Martin Luther frequently asked of a man, ". . . but does he know of death and the devil?" Amos Wilder uses the image of a reef in the open sea. "It is against the cruel and adamant ledge that the currents of the ocean disclose their phosphorescence or break into iridescent foam and spray. So it is with our finite limits, our inexorable restraints, that reveal us."

What Thomas Cranmer called "the sure and certain hope of the Resurrection unto eternal life" (*Book of Common Prayer,* p. 333) gives us the goal that empowers our wills to move out of and through the stages of infantilism, adolescence, maturity, and death at their appropriate times and breaks up the fear-driven compulsion to freeze or return. Eugene Ionesco, in his essay on Kafka, indicates what death can be when it is only the affirmation of despair. "Anything without a goal is absurd . . . when man is cut off from his religious or metaphysical roots, he is lost; all his struggles become senseless, futile and oppressive."

THE NARROW GATE INTO THE NEW LIFE

The goal of resurrection gives some confidence of purpose and a purpose in our death. It frees us from inappropriate value put on unripe fruit, on the idolatry of being

young, and allows us to appreciate, respect, and love the
wrinkles, experience, and life of man *truly* come of age.
Even in the quiet, private, unknown back eddies of history,
what this world calls "lost causes," anything that was brave,
kind, honorable, loving is not wasted or lost. This goal of
God's just peace provides a certain serenity now in the
midst of strife.

> O Lord support us all the day long
> Until the shadows lengthen
> And the evening comes,
> And the busy world is hushed,
> And the fever of life is over
> And our work is done.
> Then in thy mercy
> Grant us a safe lodging, and a holy rest,
> And peace at the last.

This is no nirvana peace, because stern judgment com-
pletes all that is not finished. What keeps this peace from
being nirvana is that goal. This "savage honesty" is an implacable enemy of all sentimentality, injustice, and sin,
but it is also that justice which declares itself in making
us just. The communist's cry, "You have nothing to lose
but your chains" is replaced here by the cry, "You have
nothing to lose but your sins (precious though they seem
to be)."

To be squeezed through that narrow gate by God's "impossible possibility" is not to lose but to gain our humanity.
John Donne knew the ultimate goodness of this judgment
and resurrection when he wrote:

As perchance, carvers do not faces make,
But that away, which hid them there, do take
Let Crosses, soe, take what hid Christ in thee,
And be his image, or not his, but hee.

The maker, carver, and carpenter of that cross is he who will be our judge.

PART THREE

Participating in the Promise

seven

KNOWING GOD IN THE AGE OF HIS "DEATH"

AT THIS point a reader might very well say: "All this about disesteem, guilt, anger and death seems accurate enough. Even the way the Christian doctrines of justification, sanctification, atonement, and resurrection seem to fit these problems is rather astonishing and even encouraging. But how do I get on board? Even if it's true, I feel as if that train just doesn't stop here anymore." Unless God is, and is knowable, all that has been written thus far is, at best, an accurate description of the problems of being human and how these problems might be met by the Christian faith, *if it were true*. Let us now attempt to deal with this issue of truth.

The Easter Bunny and Santa Claus represent the overwhelming way this age seems to look at Christianity. None of my children believes Santa Claus comes down the chimney, and my five-year-old was told by a neighbor that his mother, not the Bunny, really hides the eggs. The next step was inevitable: my twelve-year-old "found out" that God did not make trees, "the molecules did." There is little outright facing of the issues because everyone knows that Santa is a symbol of generosity and Christmas spirit. One would have to be an absolute Scrooge to be against Santa. Certainly only the most literal minded would oppose the excitement and wonder in a child's imagination concerning the visit each spring of the Easter Bunny. By extension, Jesus, too, is regarded as a symbol of religion and morals. One would be a bad actor indeed to be against *him* as a symbol of goodness. As with Santa and the Bunny we grow up and no longer believe in God acting in history. His symbols help to remind us of virtuous things. The objective details of the biblical stories are important only to children and neurotic folk who are still childish. Ansoline, in *For Whom the Bell Tolls,* expressed the spirit of these times. "We do not have God here any more, neither his son nor the Holy Ghost."

THE "DEATH" OF GOD

The term "death of God" is a technical one with varying meanings. The meaning most widely shared is that *for this age* God is dead, that the assumptions of these times preclude the possibility of knowledge of God. The radical theologians exposed to full view the belief, even within the churches, that the creeds meant no more to Christianity than the chimney and reindeer did to the spirit of Christmas.

Anyone who takes the Christian faith seriously must, first of all, face just how incredible or inaccessible God is to modern man. There is astonishing agreement among

Christians and non-Christians alike as to when this inaccessibility occurred. C. S. Lewis maintained it happened between our time and that of Jane Austen. The harsh criticism Lewis received from E. M. Forster and other Cambridge colleagues was not because he fixed the period but because he insisted on identifying himself with this untimely Christian faith. J. Hillis Miller, in his book, *The Disappearance of God*, describes the five nineteenth century writers, Browning, DeQuincey, Arnold, Hopkins, and Emily Brontë, as being "stretched on the rack of a fading transcendentalism, and could reach a precarious unity only by the most extravagant stratagems of the spirit."

Perhaps no one has described "the sea of faith" retreating in "its melancholy, long, withdrawing roar . . ." more aptly than Matthew Arnold in the last stanza of "Dover Beach" (1867):

> Ah, love let us be true
> To one another! for the world, which seems
> To lie before us like a land of dreams,
> So various, so beautiful, so new,
> Hath really neither joy, nor love, nor light,
> Nor certitude, nor peace, nor help for pain;
> And we are here as on a darkling plain
> Swept with confused alarms of struggle and flight,
> Where ignorant armies clash by night.

Conventional church people tended to dismiss Arnold's account too casually as some dark unnecessary pessimism until the bomb burst from within the church. And then laments on the "demise" of the deity went up not only in Christian circles but in Judaism and Islam as well. Others welcomed his death in the sense that he never was or at least is not any more, and have tried to make a "Christian" theology without God. In spite of a brief flurry of publicity, their undertaking has proved to be a theological dead end with ultimate meaninglessness, not to mention their encounter with all the old problems of do-it-yourself religions.

However, it is a mistake to ignore the fact that no responsible critic in the whole debate within Christianity ventures to deny the death of God, that God is "dead" in the view of the overwhelming assumptions of contemporary culture. Yet this episode has made a deeply significant contribution in that it shocked conventional people into some awareness of the radical split and accelerating contradictions between Christianity and culture, which poet, playwright, and artist have long discerned.

Sir Kenneth Clark is a good example of this split. He was narrator of the thirteen films in the series entitled *Civilisation* which were shown in England on the BBC, at the National Art Gallery to packed audiences for over two years, and all over this country on television. It is an awesome and unprecedented thing to have a marvelous tour of western civilization by such a perceptive, humane, knowledgeable, sensitive, and exciting guide as Sir Kenneth. Nothing remotely like it has ever been done before, and in book form it has reached the upper levels of the best-seller lists.

It would be as interesting and important to ask him, as anyone, where we, as a civilization, are going. He answers this for us in the last paragraph of his book:

I said at the beginning that it is lack of confidence, more than anything else, that kills a civilisation. We can destroy ourselves by cynicism and disillusion, just as effectively as by bombs. Fifty years ago W. B. Yeats, who was more like a man of genius than anyone I have ever known, wrote a famous prophetic poem.

> Things fall apart; the centre cannot hold;
> Mere anarchy is loosed upon the world,
> The blood-dimmed tide is loosed, and everywhere
> The ceremony of innocence is drowned;
> The best lack all conviction, while the worst
> Are full of passionate intensity.

Well, that was certainly true between the wars, and it damn nearly destroyed us. Is it true today? Not quite, because good people have convictions, rather too many of them. The trouble is that there is still no centre. The moral and intellectual failure of Marxism has left us with no alternative to heroic materialism, and that isn't enough. One may be optimistic, but one can't exactly be joyful at the prospect before us.

"The trouble is that there is still no centre." Heroic materialism is not enough, yet the only alternative, he notes, is Marxism, which is a failure. He does not even consider the possibility of Christianity! It is significant that he does not quote the next and last lines of Yeats' poem:

And what rough beast, its hour come round at last,
Slouches towards Bethlehem to be born?

His hope is in civilization, but it is clearly shown, especially in his treatment of the Reformation, that he does not understand that "the strength of sin is the law" (in St. Paul's terms), that the "cultural superego evokes its own destruction" (in Freud's terms), or that civilization is not the answer to man-in-the-box (in terms of this book).

Another eminently influential figure, Erich Fromm, also writes with enormous confidence of man's goodness without God:

. . . If man gives up his illusion of a fatherly God, if he faces his aloneness and insignificance in the universe, he will be like a child that has left his father's house. But it is the very aim of human development to overcome infantile fixation. Man must educate himself to face reality. If he knows that he has nothing to rely on except his own powers, he will learn to use them properly.

Here is a good example of the creed of secularism: "reality" is an indifferent cosmos and man's only resource is his "own powers"; when he acknowledges this fact, "he will learn to use them properly." Not all secularists are that optimistic; but Fromm's position is a *faith* and a *hope* and, in this sense, a *religion*.

Much the same position is implicit in John Wren-Lewis's works, except that the latter would still call his position "Christian." He insists that those in contemporary culture who center their lives on ritual, sacrament, and constant reference to some supposed plan underlying experience are neurotic. "Such a way of living is paranoid fantasy-obsession."

One of the most engaging writers among psychoanalysts is Allen Wheelis, but he, too, clearly argues that the secular faith is the only source and power available to man for dealing with the problems of being human. In *The Quest for Identity* Wheelis describes the plight of a clergyman who, being intellectually and emotionally "open," gains such "insight as will force him eventually" to relinquish belief in a personal God, in life after death, and in other of the absolutes which had guaranteed security. . . .

Whether or not he can survey the damage, salvage those elements which are sound, and build a new structure of belief depends upon the *courage, tenacity, and creative ability which he can mobilize* to meet the crisis."

The point of these illustrations (aside from showing how it throws the whole problem back into the superego) is that some of the most influential, able, and perceptive of modern authorities easily and gratuitously assume, often without the slightest doubt or hesitancy, that the only hope for man is from within "the box," or within an encapsuled and sealed history without any reference to God.

AND THE ANNIHILATION OF MAN

The consequences of this commitment for our culture are not limited, however, to theology. Nicholas Berdyaev warned us some time ago in *The End of Our Time* that "where there is no God there is no man." Wylie Sypher in *Loss of the Self in Modern Literature and Art,* and Charles Glicksburg in *Self in Modern Literature* have both described the loss of self and identity in modern man, using contemporary art forms as evidence. The death of God has left "a void at the centre of things" which shows up in all aspects of society: ethics, education, politics, medicine, and economics, but nowhere more obviously or profoundly than in novels, poetry, paintings, and plays. The optimistic humanism we find in some theologians and sociologists, as well as some of the other social scientists, is not reflected in the artists. Probably the only significant artist of the twentieth century who maintained an optimistic view of the direction of the cultural drift was Hart Crane, and he committed suicide.

Part of what we mean by "artist" is that such a person sees beneath the superficial things and discerns more deeply what the reality is. Rollo May makes an impressive witness to the predictive perception of artists by noting that what Auden, Bernstein, Camus, and Kafka had observed in the 30's and 40's did not become apparent to the psychiatric establishment until the 50's and 60's. And Theodore Roszak has accurately noted in *The Making of a Counter Culture* that "most of our social scientists, one feels, regard the introduction of poetic vision into their work in much the same way a pious monk would regard bringing a whore into the monastery." This failure to acknowledge the insight of the artist may protect the naïvely optimistic plans for society but it does not face the enormous evidence of the cry of the heart that is now coming from all art forms for something more than bread alone, for some image by which the self can resist the present pressures and the aching void. Philip Rieff sees it thus: "The question is no longer as Dostoevski put it: 'Can civilized men believe?' Rather: Can unbelieving man be civilized?"

The first step, here, then, is to consider seriously the mere possibility that the facile cultural assumption of no reality beyond the closed "box" or a closed history could be wrong. Theodore Roszak's enormous contribution to our understanding of the counter culture is, I believe, due in part to his unwillingness to specify the limits of reality:

Brown and Marcuse, you and I, most of us, perhaps all of us who must now begin to dig our way out from under the ancient and entrenched estrangements of our being: how dare *we* specify the limits of the real while we stand on this benighted side of liberation?

His chapter on the "Myth of Objective Consciousness" is, in my opinion, one of the most important contributions in decades toward a popular appreciation of a philosophy of this culture that has squeezed our humanity in a closing vise. This philosophy, in a subtle but sinister way, has distorted the "scientific method" into a snowballing technocracy which attempts to objectify everything, including human beings.

In this view one must not be committed, concerned, or subjectively involved. One must be objective, aloof, detached, and disengaged. Trust, passion, care, joy, and ethical responsibility are not "scientific." Michael Polanyi, among others, has pointed out that this is not the scientific method by which science arose. When it is applied to the humanities and social sciences (stemming, in part, from the desire to upgrade their status to the "scientific") it becomes tragically dehumanizing. It is Polanyi who seems to have coined the most helpful term, "reductionism."

OUR FALSE SCIENTISM

To treat man as merely the product of sexual determinism is "psychological reductionism." To see man as merely a factor in economic forces could be called "Marxist reductionism." To explain Hamlet as merely an example of the Oedipus complex could be termed "Freudian reductionism." To study man by merely objective means is "epistemological reductionism." This antiseptic, spectator, uninvolved, depersonalized means of knowledge is "scientistic reductionism" (to put together Roszak's and Polanyi's terms).

Roszak sees a revolt against this dehumanizing establishment culture on the part of the younger generation as *The Making of a Counter-Culture*. It is a far more substantial work than the more popular *Greening of America* by Charles Reich, and not nearly so uncritically approving of anything that is young as Margaret Mead's *Culture and Commitment*. In fact, not even Floyd Matson's excellent work *The Broken Image* is as far ranging or has the urgency implicit in Roszak's statement on the dehumanizing effects of technological reductionism. Roszak insists that this younger dissident generation senses that

. . . when the mechanistic imperative has been successfully internalized as the prevailing life style of our society, we shall find ourselves moving through a world of perfected bureaucrats, managers, operations analysts, and social engineers who will be indistinguishable from the cybernated systems they assist. Already we find these images of internally deadened human beings appearing in our contemporary novels and films. Dispassionate lovers, dispassionate killers fill the movies of Godard, Truffant, Antonioni, Fellini with their blank gaze and automatized reactions. So too in the absurdist plays of Harold Pinter and Samuel Beckett we find the logical—or rather psychological—conclusion of life dominated by ruthless depersonalization. . . . [Even C. P. Snow who gave us the notion of the two cultures] scarcely grasps the terrible pathos that divides these two cultures; nor for that matter do most of our social scientists and scientistic (sic) humanists. While art and literature of our time tell us with ever more desperation that the disease from which our age is dying is that of alienation, the sciences, in their relentless pursuit of objectivity, raise alienation to its apotheosis as our *only* means of achieving a valid relationship to reality. Objective consciousness *is* alienated life promoted to its most honorific status as the scientific method.

Under its auspices we subordinate nature to our command only by estranging ourselves from more and more of what we experience, until the reality about which objectivity tells us so much finally becomes a universe of congealed alienation. It is totally within our intellectual and technical power . . . and it is a worthless possession. For "what does it profit a man that he should gain the whole world, but lose his soul?"

This false concept of the "scientific method," which Roszak so keenly perceives, threatens to destroy what is peculiarly human in our culture. Within the Christian church it has had an unfortunate influence, the most crucial area being biblical studies. I have a colleague who still has in his notes from seminary days the authoritative direction from his teacher to skip and ignore the Elihu speeches in the Book of Job because modern scholarship has shown them to be a later addition to the original. There is no question but that the Book of Job is a very early work and of non-Jewish origin. The professor was quite right that the Elihu speeches were later additions. But he was decidedly wrong in thereby eliminating them because they were later insertions. His injunction was an example not of biblical criticism but of critical literalism. In fact, because the holy folk, the people of Israel, took this story into their own tradition it is particularly important to examine and appreciate what they understood to be a necessary addition in order to bring the story into line with their experience of God. Hence, it could be argued that the Elihu speeches are as crucial as any in the story!

Putting the story of the woman taken in adultery in a small-type footnote in a modern translation of the Bible is another example of such critical literalism, whose criteria for revelation slides more and more exclusively toward the depersonalized objectivity of sources. This is to ignore the whole personal response which is necessary for understanding the Bible and which guided its compilation in the first place.

Norman O. Brown's criticism of literalism cuts both against making words the WORD (the tendency of conventional fundamentalism) and against the reductionism of critical literalism. He quotes a passage from Kazantzakis' novel, *The Last Temptation of Christ*:

> You said, "First came the wings and then the angel." We never noticed these words in Scripture, Holy Abbot.
> How could you have noticed them? Alas, your minds are still dim. You open the prophets and your eyes are able to see nothing but the letters. But what can the letters say? They are the black bars of the prison where the spirit strangles itself with screaming. Between the letters and the lines, and all around the blank margins, the spirit circulates freely; and I circulate with it and bring you this great message: Friars, first came the wings and then the angel! (p. 196.)

This misunderstanding of the scientific method, which both Roszak and Brown see as deleterious to our culture, also inhibits modern Christians from becoming recipients of the experience of God's revelation. It needs to be understood in its origin and disentangled from its legitimate background to avoid an antiscience posture or even a regression to magic. No one has traced the gradual and historical distortion of the scientific method in simpler terms than the great mathematician and self-consciously non-Christian philosopher, Bertrand Russell.

Science in its beginnings was due to men who were in love with the world. . . . They were men of Titanic passionate intellect, and from the intensity of their intellectual passion the whole movement of the modern world has sprung. But step by step, as science has developed, the impulse of love which gave it birth has been increasingly thwarted, while the impulse of power, which was at first a mere camp-follower, has gradually usurped command in virtue of its unforeseen success. The lover of nature has been baffled, the tyrant over nature has been rewarded. As physics has developed, it has deprived us step by step of what we thought we knew concerning the intimate nature of the physical world. Colour and sound, light and shade, form and texture, belong no longer to that external nature that the Ionians sought as the bride of their devotion. All these things have been transferred from the beloved to the lover, and the beloved has become a skeleton of rattling bones, cold and dreadful, but perhaps a mere phantasm. . . . Disappointed as the lover of nature, the man of science is becoming its tyrant. What matters it, says the practical man, whether the outer world exists or is a dream, provided I can make it behave as I wish? Thus science has more and more substituted power-knowledge for love-knowledge, and as this substitution becomes completed science tends more and more to become sadistic. The scientific society of the future as we have been imagining it is one in which the power impulse has completely overwhelmed the impulse of love, and this is the psychological source of the cruelties which it is in danger of exhibiting.

Copernicus and Pascal loved what they did and their scientific contributions were not in spite of, but because of, the intensity and passion of their intellect. William Derham in 1713 said that the infinite mechanism of a spider's eye thrilled him as much as did the orderly motion of the planets. Indeed he climaxed an essay on insects exclaiming, "O infinitely Great God, I am astonished! I am astonished!"

One of the milestones in this step-by-step deprivation that Russell outlines was John Locke. It was he who insisted that "Colour and sound, light and shade, form and texture" no longer belonged to the external world but were only the secondary qualities in the mind of the beholder. It is astonishing how poets like W. B. Yeats have understood this connection between scientific philosophy and the ambiguities of the industrial revolution, even to its effect upon the sexes. Seeing a new Adam and a new Eve in another story of a more modern "Fall" he wrote:

> Locke sank into a swoon;
> The Garden died;
> God took the spinning-jenny
> Out of his side.

The contemporary ecological crisis was predicted and its causes explained by Bertrand Russell almost fifty years ago.

Science, which began as the pursuit of truth, is becoming incompatible with veracity, since complete veracity tends more and more to complete scientific scepticism. When science is considered contemplatively, not practically, we find that what we believe, we believe owing to animal faith, and it is only our disbeliefs that are due to science. When, on the other hand, science is considered as a technique for the transformation of ourselves and our environment it is found to give us a power quite independent of its metaphysical validity. But we can only wield this power by ceasing to ask ourselves metaphysical questions as to the nature of reality. Yet these questions are the evidence of a lover's attitude towards the world. Thus it is only in so far as we renounce the world as its lovers that we can conquer it as its technicians. But this division in the soul is fatal to what is best in man. As soon as the failure of science considered as metaphysics is realized the power conferred by science as a technique is only obtainable by something analogous to the worship of Satan, that is to say, by the renunciation of love.

The key here is Russell's accurate insistence that asking ourselves the metaphysical (beyond physical) questions of reality are the "evidence of a lover's attitude towards the world." It is uncanny that Eugene Ionesco sees and shows this same diagnosis in his play *The Chairs*. In a letter to the director he points to the crucial issue in the play:

The subject of the play is not the message, nor the failures of life, nor the moral disaster of the two old people, but the chairs themselves; that is to say, the absence of people, the absence of the emperor, the absence of God, the absence of matter, the unreality of the world, *metaphysical emptiness* (italics mine). The theme of the play is *nothingness*. . . .

This metaphysical emptiness is what seals twentieth-century man in his box and as long as it is accepted it precludes the possibility of revelation, of the experience of God. We shall see later how this false model of knowledge, this dehumanizing passion for objectifying technology, this flight from the metaphysical questions, this "myth of objective consciousness" can be replaced by a means of seeing, hearing, and knowing that is personalizing and humanizing. But first we must take up the second barrier of our modern block concerning God. It is the charge against Christianity of *infantilism*.

"INFANTILISM"—REALLY?

The charge that Christianity nurtures infantilism is an exceedingly serious one and has so pervaded our culture that even children who have never heard of Freud assume that belief in God is perhaps a childish weakness on the part of those who still want some heavenly parent to take care of them. It's almost as if some grown-ups still believe in Santa Claus! The dynamics are roughly as follows: as we grow older we perceive not only in ourselves, but, with some real shock, in our parents, the impotence to cope with many aspects of life. A normal growth would move from the infant's belief in his mother's absolute omnipotence, through the child's opinion that his father can lick any man on the block, to the adolescent's usually painful adjustment to the discovery of the clay feet of both parents, to a mature adult's recognition and acceptance of the fact of human frailties, including his own.

However, few of us have a smooth transition through those stages. Many, who are unable to accept the reality of a father powerless in the face of much in this strange world, freeze and are unable to move toward maturity. Instead we project into the heavens a Father who is not powerless but knows all, can do all, and takes care of us all. The church, seen in this light, is thus a community of neurotic people who, being unable to move toward maturity, band together in a common illusion that there is a Father who made us, takes care of us, and will bring us back to himself when we die. This is seen to be not only a wish-ful-filling fantasy, a neurotic projection, and a cultic illusion, but a positively unhygienic enterprise that nurtures people in their infantilism and inhibits their maturity.

This popular idea has rested largely (but not altogether) on Freud's *The Future of an Illusion* published in 1927. Yet it is a measure of the secular tide's power to contrast the scrupulous restraint with which Freud himself spoke of the term "illusion" with the more recent casually assumed dogmatisms of Erich Fromm, Allen Wheelis, and John Wren-Lewis. Freud himself very carefully limited his meaning of illusion to a special psychological sense and added, "It does not lie within the scope of this inquiry to estimate the value of religious doctrines as truth."

Dr. Roy S. Lee makes the important distinction that Freud understood. Psychoanalysis "may challenge the truth or adequacy of assertions about fact made in the guise of religion, or of assumptions on which religious doctrines are based, or it may question the factual interpretation of a particular religious experience, such as a vision, but as psychoanalysis it cannot pronounce on the ultimate truth and validity of religion." Freud could still make the distinction between physics and psychoanalysis on the one hand and metaphysics and ontology on the other. He did not pretend to be dealing with the latter, but the tide, so eloquently described above by Russell, has swept away from modern consciousness all thought of what is beyond (meta) the physical reality and what underlies (ontology or the study of being) what we observe. Hence, the charge of "illusion" against Christianity is not merely one that criticizes its neurotic manifestations but goes to the heart of Christian revelation.

Two things must be admitted at the outset. There is absolutely no question but that the Christian church has sometimes done exactly what its enemies charge. In authoritarian and tyrannical ways responsibility has been usurped from church people and they have been treated as children and nurtured in their infantile subjection. In moral theology a long and infamous tradition exists which puts every premium possible on persons relinquishing their responsibility for a dependent relationship with authority. There has been Protestant obscurantism, Catholic coercion, medieval tyranny, and ancient superstition. However, that is only the small and ugly part of a much greater picture.

The second thing that must be confessed is that I personally believe it is quite possible for otherwise intelligent people to believe *anything* if they are desperate enough. This is not an opinion I am confident of sharing with the general reader, but I believe anyone with any significant clinical or pastoral experience is overwhelmingly impressed with the ability of people to "hear" what they want to hear and "see" what they desperately need to see. I remember once telling an eleven-year-old boy that his father had died. He replied by telling me about the circus. I told him again about his father and he told me about a clown on a bicycle. He did not want to hear and, at least temporarily, did not. I must add to the seriousness of the charge against Christianity of infantile projection that I personally believe it could be possible for men to make up, out of nothing, a whole cogent system whose only relation to reality would be their own neurotic need.

At some point everyone must do his own believing. Let us take the charge seriously, without making a straw man of it, and run it through the scripture to see how credible it is. Each person can then make up his own mind. Let us start with Abraham. Frozen in some neurotic way he projected onto the heavens a voice that called him out of the land he knew into a land he did not know. That does not comfortably fit with infantile characteristics which balk at new situations and tend to remain in or return to what is familiar. One would have expected Abraham to hear the Father tell him to stay, remain, or go back.

Moses heard a call telling him to go back to the danger of Egypt from which he had escaped and to free his people. Infants don't usually hear calls to danger. My five-year-old son never seems to be called upstairs by himself when it's dark, much less into some dangerous Egypt. Also, the content of the call is a strange thing to fit into an infantile echo: "Go and free my people." These people in the wilderness believed that God gave Moses the ten commandments, and this celestial parent they have made up has most inconveniently walled them around with astonishing restrictions and expressly forbidden what is precisely desired by infants: to have their own way. The prophet Micah, shall we say, bounces off the unanswering heavens his own childish desires, ". . . and what doth the Lord require of thee, but to do justly and to love mercy, and to walk humbly with thy God?" The substance of the echo is, from any neutral position, anything but infantile. One could imagine demands for justice, but to couple them with mercy is not a characteristic of childishness or neurosis. To combine justice and mercy and then to add humility is not typical of the ideals of most adults.

It is interesting to increase the odds against Christianity by upping the charge from infantilism to adolescence. If there is anything characteristic of a certain adolescent stage it is fascination with Superman. Whoever started it knew the wish in adolescence for external power. The Superman syndrome proliferates, touching everything for that age from Atom Man to Mighty Mouse. It takes some measure of real growth as a person to become bored with Superman.

Could Isaiah's hope for the Suffering Servant who would heal the divisions in men's hearts be regarded as adolescent, much less infantile? It is difficult in my house even to get the table set. Is it likely that a child would project wishes for a servant for all men to follow as servants? Could immature people even imagine that only suffering servanthood would heal the hurt and antagonism among us? Isaiah's profound, costly, and heart-changing hope is scarcely a childish projection.

The most mature adults still expend enormous energies in justifying themselves and find it exceedingly difficult to accept a judgment that in the slightest aspect denies their understanding of righteousness. And yet we are asked to believe that Job made up out of his unconscious infantile neurosis the echo from the Father: "Gird up thy loins now like a man: I will demand of thee . . . wilt thou condemn me, that thou mayest be righteous?" (Job 40:7–8) It is much more likely that it would have come back: "Let me tuck you in like a child and keep you safe from those who are wrong, because you are right."

Amos, Hosea, Jeremiah and Ezekiel all hear the word of the Lord that places responsibility in the lap of Israel and individuals. They do not prophesy smooth things, as fantasies do, but demand and disclose a justice and hard goodness. If that is called infantile and neurotic it would turn upside down the meaning of all words and require us to believe the infinitely improbable on no evidence at all.

THE CRUCIAL QUESTION

The crucial issue, however, is in facing Jesus. "What think ye of Christ?" Nothing is as disappointing as his refusal to fulfill our adolescent wishes. He did not grant the childish desire to overthrow all with his might and bring in his kingdom by coercion. He did not punish the wicked (them) and reward the righteous (us). All have sinned: you, me, Freud, and Fromm. He makes us new by a life lived, loved, suffered, and terminated by death. Such a life is not congruent with infantile hopes, whether of a five- or fifty-year-old. The infantile cry of the people at Pilate's court was, "Give us Barabbas!" Only those who matured under Jesus' teaching were able to see him as Lord. Only those who had so seen him could recognize him at his resurrection.

The charge that Christianity is a projection of infantile desires could be much more cogently reversed. Edward Stein points out in *Guilt: Theory and Therapy*:

It is possible that the underlying and perhaps unconscious motivation for the "God is dead" theology is pride, man's continued infantile desire to replace the father (God) and to be *more* than a son and creature and, further, extrapolation from the Oedipal aggression incident upon man's socialization—his murderous wish to eliminate the father as an obstacle to his incestuous fusion with nature (an escape from the anxiety of freedom) as he experiences such security in the mother figure. . . . This return to mother to escape reality (and father, god) is possible to conceive incestuously or idolatrously. The Biblical writers frequently equate idolatry and harlotry. In any case it is a "disobedient" regression from responsible mature growth.

Modern man's ego makes a binding effort to unite himself directly with reality (seen in reverse forms of regression to orgiastic rites, chemical religions such as LSD, etc.) and represents a short cut which would seek to leave out father as a necessary polar element in the male-female (androgynous) fundamentals of self which constitute the irreducible minimum poles of complete personality.

Professor Stein helps us understand why there are those who do not want God because they see him as threatening the short-cut to their hope of "home," that is, nature. Norman O. Brown wishes for a oneness with nature unfettered by any accountability to God. When Adam is asked in the Garden, "Where art thou?", Brown counters, "Let there be no one to answer to." *Love's Body*, p. 88.

Where is the infantilism? We have seen the Christian answer to disesteem/self-hatred as a state of forgiveness grounded on a righteousness not our own. Building on this foundation of "no condemnation," the discontent of guilt is transformed into the persistent pull toward a health and humanity we have not yet known. The agony of anger destructively seeking scapegoats is buried in the Lamb who gives us back responsibility we have tried to displace. The shadow of death is penetrated by the light of the sure and certain hope, the savage honesty of resurrection, where we are answerable to a justice not our own. This is the claim and experience of Christians. Is this infantilism? Everyone must do his own believing.

To appropriate the revelation in Christ, "to get on board," we must first hurdle these two barriers to modern belief: scientistic reductionism and the charge of infantilism. There is only one way to overlap these barriers, "to get on board." It has been before our eyes but continually overlooked. One of the reasons why we have not seen it is because it is hidden underneath layers of distortion and obscured by constant misuse. It is *pistis,* or as we translate to English, *faith.*

FAITH AS KNOWLEDGE AND GROWTH

Faith is both the means of knowledge and the means of growth. Faith carries with it all the distinctly human aspects of knowing: trust, involvement, caring, commitment, and affirmation. It exists on a different level from mere physical perception. Many people knew Jesus on such a level; they recognized his features and knew him to be the son of Joseph and Mary. But only his disciples, who knew him on a level deeper than mere physical observation, could see him as "my Lord and my God." The hard fact is that God is known only through what is peculiarly human and personal. One does not know a Spirit by dispassionate, uninvolved, impersonal, detached observation. With eyes inferior to those God gave a buzzard we can easily measure and record the weight of a football player. But it takes imagination, perception, and insight to recognize the spirit which characterizes a football team. With ears inferior to those given an opossum a mother is able to hear her son come in at night. But to hear what he is saying when he is sullen and silent requires a peculiarly human attribute, a heart. (Obviously I am not talking about a pump that moves blood around a carcass, but that which symbolizes the center of personhood.) I have a blind friend who frequently "sees" more in a person's voice than I observe in the person's whole appearance.

A close friend once asked me if I knew a certain Oxford dean. "Yes," I replied, "I knew that rude, gruff, and insensitive man." My friend was surprised by my negative view and when I explained to him what I had observed on several occasions he laughed and said, "Yes, that is quite typical of him. He would do that sort of thing. But you don't really know him." My friend went on to tell me another side of that man, about his compassion, vulnerability, and sensitivity to other people's hurt. In order to protect himself from this all too tender side he would erect an exceedingly gruff, clipped, business-like exterior. This is what I had seen. My friend, in a period of desperate trouble, I learned, had been taken into the dean's home as a son and there he saw (not as an eye observes but as a son sees) and came to know this man whom I had only observed. In fact, my friend went on to describe him in ways that introduced me to him. I came to know him 3,000 miles away, a year after I had observed him, and even after he had died.

Although a historian by vocation, I shall go to the grave without being worthy of tying the shoes of Charles Beard or Christopher Dawson. Yet I know Martin Luther far better than they. Neither of them (for quite different reasons) shared the concerns of Luther. It was neither the expanse of time nor the weakness of the documents concerning Luther that set the barrier between him and them. They observed Luther as I first observed the dean mentioned above. The will to see the side of Luther which enables me to know him so much more intimately was not given to them.

Professor Hugh Trevor-Roper introduced me to a side of Erasmus that was inaccessible to me because I am not as sympathetic with Erasmus as he. I do not believe Trevor-

Roper would care to call himself a Christian. The beliefs of Erasmus are enough for him; they are not enough for me. Yet I think Trevor-Roper's essay on Erasmus is one of the finest essays on any subject by anyone in this generation. It is clear from his preface where Trevor-Roper's heart is, and his passion, commitment, and involvement are the indispensable means by which Erasmus is known.

There are, then, things in science, sports, love-making, scholarship, fishing, cooking, acting, and every human activity that become inaccessible when reduced to quantitative and impersonal means of knowledge. This is what Roszak means in criticizing the objective consciousness. This is what is wrong with both biblical and critical literalism. The experience and revelation of God is, similarly, accessible only to peculiarly human means of knowledge. Buzzards see and opossums hear better than men. The crowd in Jerusalem could see and hear Jesus. Only his disciples could see and hear who Jesus is. What did they see and hear with? They saw and heard with the same organs with which Helen Keller, who was permanently deaf and blind from infancy, saw and heard—the heart and the will. Anyone who has read anything of Helen Keller's life or has seen the superb play *The Miracle Worker* knows that this blind and deaf woman has seen and heard far more of what is humanly important than many people with normal healthy eyes and ears.

D. H. Lawrence correctly observes that "we moderns are captives not of regimes but of our own lust for reasoning from the outside in." The influence of scientistic reductionism within our secular culture has made it surprising to most of us how astonishingly few "outside" miracles there are in scripture. Most of the wonders in scripture, and certainly the most crucially important, are the "inside" miracles discerned only by faith.

Elijah did not hear God in the earthquake, wind, or fire but "after the fire a still small voice." (I Kings 19:12) The *Jerusalem Bible* translates this, "the sound of a gentle breeze." Another possible translation is that the voice of God was heard "in the pregnant silence." No matter how it is translated, it was the kind of voice accessible to the peculiarly human means of knowing that said, "What are you doing here, Elijah?" The Spirit descended on Jesus at his baptism *"like* a dove." (Mk. 1:10) (Matt. 3:16) The Spirit came at Pentecost *"as* of a rushing mighty wind" (Acts 2:2) and tongues *"like as* to fire." (Acts 2:3) Jesus's sweat in Gethsemane "was *as it were* great drops of blood." (Lk. 22:44)

It is interesting how many times in Jesus's healing ministry his observation is "thy faith hath made thee whole." (Mk. 5:34, 10:52; Lk. 8:48, 17:19) The wonders of scripture are seen and discerned by faith, by attributes of personhood that are on a level other than those of eye and ear. The involvement, hope ("Faith is the substance of the things hoped for, the evidence of things unseen." Heb. 11:1), courage, imagination, commitment, trust, and passion are always the means of truly knowing another person, or even knowing nature on levels beneath appearances and externals.

The English theologian L. P. Jacks once observed, "We see with our wills." The disciples who walked, talked, and fished with Jesus only began to see him clearly as their wills became engaged with his teaching and person. And then they knew him more fully in his betrayal, crucifixion, and death. They saw him more fully in his resurrection and

knew him again "in the breaking of bread." (Lk. 24:35)
As I only observed and did not truly know the Oxford dean
until I was physically removed from him in both time
and space, so our Lord's disciples did not fully know the
Christ until their wills were turned so that they could see
with them.

We not only see with our wills but we hear with our
hearts. How could Helen Keller become such a profound
Christian when she was physically deaf and could not hear
the WORD? Through her teacher, Ann Sullivan, this
blind, deaf, mute, almost animal child was pulled, sometimes kicking and screaming, into the human world. There,
Helen Keller, in spite of her handicaps, graduated *cum
laude* from Radcliffe and wrote more than a dozen books.

Often overlooked was the miracle of Ann Sullivan. Could
you imagine anything being accomplished if she had taken
the role of scientistic detachment, emotional uninvolvement,
dispassionate observation, or professional objectivity? Instead, like the early scientists whom Bertrand Russell described, she had a passionate intensity that alone could
have broken down the wall between them. Helen Keller
heard through the only organ available to her, her heart,
and Ann Sullivan spoke to her with the only organ that
could have communicated, her own heart.

"Wherefore be ye not unwise (foolish), but understanding what the will of the Lord is." (Eph. 5:17) The
original word here for unwise or foolish (*aphrontes*) has
the meaning of being unhooked from "the midriff or diaphragm, the parts about the heart; the mind; the faculty of
perceiving and judging." The word for understanding
"what the will of the Lord is" (*sunientes*) means "with it"
and not alongside of it as a stranger. It is to put things to-

gether or "to put (as it were) the perception with the thing perceived; to set or join together in the mind."

This is what Ann Sullivan did. She was not so foolish as to have her eyes and ears dissociated from her heart and she understood Helen Keller by being with her, not along-side as a stranger. But that is not the direction much teaching, knowing, and learning follows in today's culture. It is now as Jesus said then, "Seeing they do not see, and hearing they do not hear, nor do they understand." (Matt. 13:13).

Hence, Christian revelation frustrates and disappoints the expectations of both scientistic reductionism and infan-tile longings. Both converge in the demand for God to disclose himself on our terms, which is the safety of ex-ternals and a childish reluctance to be stretched in maturity. He answers with his awesome silence. The stature of the fullness of man requires growth not in pounds but in will, not in height but in heart. The media of his revelation is at the same time the media of our growth: our wills and our hearts. This is why Christianity talks of feeding on the Word. In discerning and hearing the word of God we are nurtured and fed for a fuller humanity. "Man does not live by bread alone, but by every word of God." (Lk. 4:4)

I find it comforting that the record of our Lord's prayers in Gethsemane gives no picture of some external tape-recordable answers from the Father. God has always left unanswered my scientistic and infantile expectations, pull-ing and stretching me with disappointments for which I've been deeply grateful in retrospect. Even for Jesus the an-swer to prayer was not easily objectified and externalized. In fact, it is recorded that he prayed three times in great agony concerning the cup. (Matt. 26:39–44) Some Bibles have the words of Jesus printed in red type and the narrative in black. It is interesting to note that there is no gold type with the words of the Father recorded: "Look, son, as I told you earlier this morning, you don't have to worry because it'll be just two days." We have no picture of Jesus having written down notes from the Father and, when near despair on the cross, reading the reassuring message taken down the night before.

"Verily thou art a God that hidest thyself, O God of Israel, the Saviour." (Isaiah 45:15) William Porcher Du-Bose, pointed out many years ago how the law can function in Christianity in such a way as to help Christians to see and use their secular experience.

It is a necessary part of the evolution of a true manhood that it should learn both its independence and its dependence upon God. . . . The design and result of the law was thus a double one, to teach at once the necessity and the impossibility of a personal human righteousness. Man only becomes man by asserting himself in his freedom against an environment of mere nature and necessity, but equally he only becomes himself by surrendering the freedom so asserted to the personal will and wisdom that is above nature and necessity. But it is characteristic of a system of mere divine law and not grace that it casts man off upon himself; it requires of him to become himself in and by himself and so, beginning with building him up in his independence, ends by casting him down in the discovery and consciousness of his utter dependence. It might be said that it is the method of God to unchild men by nature in order to make them his children by grace, to cast them upon themselves so as to compel them to come back to him of themselves, to want and seek him through faith, and to become anew his children by the higher personal bond of mutual love—for so alone could the natural, necessary, immanental relation and dependence of all things alike upon God pass up into the free, filial, spiritual relation and dependence of finite personalities upon the infinite divine Person.

In the same way our common secular experience of the death of God breaks our infantile ties and leaves us humbled in the face of the "necessity and the impossibility of a personal human righteousness." Now is opened up the new, mature, personal, and free possibility of our utter dependence on Him.

The train has stopped and is awaiting all who, no longer trusting in their own righteousness, can begin to see and hear as finite men.

eight

FINDING IDENTITY IN WORSHIP

IN THE history of timely terms and trite sayings there is scarcely one which has caught on as rapidly and widely as the term "identity crisis." Even Erik Erikson, who is credited with coining the term, protests its shallow and faddist extensions. However, terms never become trite without containing some important truth or meeting some urgent need. Identity crisis in twentieth-century culture places an additional weight on the normal and perennial identity crisis of each man in each age.

An age for which God is dead, is without the assumption upon which the image of man has historically been built. Christian civilization had woven into its literature, institutions, and unconscious memory the assertion that man is made in the image of God. Now with this assertion rejected, the image of man has become more and more acutely up for grabs. Hence, there has arisen the overwhelming (and sometimes tiresome) theme of modern art and cry on the contemporary campus: "Who am I?"

It is a good question, an exceedingly important one to ask and answer. Bishop Stephen Bayne has put it this way:

That we may see man as he is, single and whole, reasoning and choosing and believing, half of this world and half of some other, the only animal who must decide what kind of animal he will be, the only beast it is shameful to call a beast, whose soul, as Boethius said, "Albeit in a cloudy memory, yet seeks back his own good, but like a drunken man knows not the way home."

John Updike's character in *The Centaur*, George Caldwell, climaxes his lecture on evolution with the appearance of "the flint-chipping, fire-kindling, death-foreseeing, tragic animal called 'man'." The Psalmist asks, "What is man, that thou art mindful of him?" (8:4) Some see man's almost infinite capacity for misery and others see his majestic capacity for grandeur. Only a few, like Blaise Pascal, have seen both his grandeur and his misery.

A thirty-five-year-old lady once told me she had been crying for two days. "I'm a wife, mother, daughter, car pool driver, and secretary of the P.T.A., but I don't know who I am." Although she was asking the question, she was receiving no satisfactory answer. The important point is that each of us asks and answers this question about identity on some level, often unconsciously.

CONTEMPORARY IMAGES OF MAN

Esquire magazine carried an article (August, 1970) entitled "The Church of our Children." On the cover was pictured a Gothic church just recently converted into a movie theatre, with the marquee billing: "Easy Rider." The point of the article was that movies today are replacing the churches as sources for religious integration in this younger generation. This has been said many times before but the article aptly disclosed the religious nature of what is too frequently seen only as entertainment. I have a friend who has seen *Cool Hand Luke* nine times and another *The Graduate* seven times.

Here are the images by which the often unconscious questions of identity are being answered. The culture has long ago recognized this function of image-making by calling some actors matinee idols. Everyone has always resolved his identity questions by parents, surrogate mother or father figures, saints, heroes, royalty, leaders, or stars of theatre and sports.

How we, you and I, work out our identities between the pressures of civilization and nature is crucially important. No one escapes doing it, for it is a universal problem. Men know they must die and alone among the animals, are able to some small extent, to look back consciously at themselves. Men alone must choose the images to shape and mold their identities. We have seen, however, that many of our choices are served up subtly and are made unconsciously. Many human problems of identity can be "solved" by choosing some animal model (Chapter 2), and the image of the machine in a technological culture (Chapter 7) can have insidious effects upon modern man's identity. Roszak gives us a keen insight into the religious nature of making the machine the savior of a technological society.

So we come to the ultimate irony: the machine which is a creature of the human being becomes—most fully in the form of the computerized process—its maker's ideal. The machine achieves the perfect state of objective consciousness and, hence, becomes the standard by which all things are to be gauged. It embodies the myth of objective consciousness as Jesus incarnated the Christian conception of divinity. Under its spell a grand reductive process begins in which culture is redesigned to meet the needs of mechanization. If we discover that a computer cannot compose emotionally absorbing music, we insist that music does have an "objective" side, and we turn that into our definition of music. If we discover that computers cannot translate normal language, then we invent special, more rudimentary language which they can translate. If we discover that computers cannot teach as teaching at its most ideal is done, then we redesign education so that the machine can qualify as a teacher. If we discover that computers cannot solve the basic problems of city planning—all of which are questions of social philosophy and aesthetics—then we redefine the meaning of "city," call it an "urban area," and assume that all the problems of this entity are quantitative. In this way man is replaced in all areas by the machine, not because the machine can do things "better," but rather because all things have been reduced to what the machine is capable of doing.

An alternative source to machines and animals from which we can derive images for our identity is a combination of other people. Yet we all can recognize, especially in others, the debilitating and damaging effect of someone attempting to be the person that he is not. There is a time, for example, when a father represents for his child what it means to be a man; but the time comes when his image is no longer sufficient, a time when the son must go beyond . . . but to what?

Maurice Friedman has given us some searching and far-reaching answers to that question in two books: *The Problematic Rebel: An Image of Modern Man* and *To Deny Our Nothingness: Contemporary Images of Man*. These works give an eloquent account of the unfortunate effects of man's understanding himself by the models of Marx, Freud, linguistic analysis, or Greek tragedy. But Friedman shows the inevitable necessity of man's choosing some image by which he can understand what his self is. Believing, as Friedman does, that God is in no way now accessible to man, we do not have Job's option of dialogue with God.

The only hope left, then, according to Friedman, of avoiding the dehumanizing effects of subtle models and images which are less than man, is to take the best images and open ourselves to them "to deny our nothingness." For Friedman these images are figures from existential literature: Ahab and Ishmael from Melville; Alyosha, Dmitri, and Ivan from Dostoievski; "K" from Kafka's *The Castle,* and Dr. Rieux from Camus' *The Plague.* These seven figures (with some qualifications) form the mosaic pattern modern man must hold up before him to esteem and venerate, and by which to understand his nature. Friedman asserts that this solution to the crisis of identity will save us from the destructive and dehumanizing effects of the alternative images of man which reduce him to the level of a thing or an animal.

The title of Friedman's second book comes from a quotation of André Malraux: "The greatest mystery is not that we have been flung at random among the profusion of the earth and the galaxy of the stars, but that in this prison we can fashion images of ourselves sufficiently powerful *to deny our nothingness.*"

WORSHIP AS A CHOICE OF IMAGES

Let us make no mistake, fashioning images of ourselves to deny our nothingness is worship. Friedman never uses the word, and conventional church definitions of worship would not help us recognize its presence in what he is proposing. However, this is precisely what scripture means by worship: man's fashioning images to overcome his nothingness. The consistent biblical claim is that man was made in the image of God and when he takes something finite out of creation, or fashions for himself something finite to serve as the image by which he understands himself, that is idolatry.

The children of Israel got tired of waiting for Moses to bring down the commandments of God, and not enduring this eclipse or apparent death of God, they fashioned unto themselves a golden calf as an image to give themselves vitality, a potency, to overcome their nothingness. We think, "How silly of such primitive people to make a golden calf," but let us look more closely. First of all, it was not merely a calf, it was a bull, a young bull. Secondly, "the people sat down to eat and to drink, and rose up to play. . . . And when Moses saw that the people were naked. . . ." (Ex. 32:6–25) This is neither merely primitive nor silly. Our twentieth-century literature is saturated with images to arouse sexual potency and crammed with examples where the crisis of identity is resolved by sex. Sex and the Greek god Eros have not ceased to seduce humans into the religious hope that man's identity can be established by some "simultaneous passion."

Pray for us, enchanted with
The green Bohemia of that myth
Where knowledge of the flesh can take
The guilt of being born away,
Simultaneous passions make
One eternal chastity:
Pray for us romantics, pray.

It is unfortunate that the concept of worship has been interpreted so narrowly, swept, so to speak, into an ecclesiastical ghetto. Most church people think of worship as simply a Sunday morning exercise. They are encouraged in this by a professionalized liturgical and devotional emphasis which is neither biblical nor secular in its meaning of worship. Evelyn Underhill, to cite one instance, defined worship as: "the response of the creature to the Eternal" and "the acknowledgement of the Transcendent" and it "always means God and the priority of God."

Worship in scripture was not by any means always a "response to the Eternal." It too often meant quite the opposite: the fashioning of images that were not God and thus idols. The Hebrew people knew that "they that make them [idols] are like unto them; and so are all they that put their trust in them." (Ps. 135:18) The fundamental dynamic is that you become like what you worship. If man is created in the image of God, nothing less than God can reflect man's true self. When he finds or fashions something less than God to reflect his image, to rely on, to hope for, to see himself by, to overcome his nothingness with, he will drag himself down to levels beneath what is truly human. There is nothing in creation (or within "the box") that will not diminish man if used as a model for his identity.

Such non-Christians as Roszak and Friedman teach us more of the dangerously dehumanizing effect of assuming cultural models and images for our identity than conventional church authorities on worship. What is badly needed is a definition of worship that will bring it out of the ecclesiastical ghetto into the world we live in, where the crucial issues of identity are being resolved, for good or ill.

Worship is the inevitable conscious and unconscious choosing of images (or models) to resolve the crisis of identity. It is the affirmation of, the trust in, and the opening of oneself to that by which one hopes to know what it means to be human.

The first point to notice about this definition is that it is universal and confined neither to church nor to Christianity. All men inevitably put their trust in something by which they hope to know their identity or what it means to be human. The second point about this definition is that it is biblical. The word *therapeuo* is one we translate *worship.* It means to serve, cure, heal. That which we serve and hope for our health and wholeness is what we worship. Another is *doxa* meaning glory or esteem. That to which we attribute highest respect or esteem, we worship. Another is *sebomai* meaning to venerate. That which we respect to the level of veneration, we worship. Another is *proskuneo* meaning to kiss the hand toward, to appear before in postures of humility and service, to kneel before and bow down to. That before which we humble ourselves tends to shape our destiny and nature. As A. D. Weisman has so well stated: "What we idealize determines what we believe controls the universe and what we strive to emulate."

It is also the way newspapers, magazines, and shoptalk deal with worship. When some golfer has attained such fame (*doxa*—worth) and is so venerated (*sebomai*) that he makes more money modeling clothes and selling clubs than he does playing golf, he is called a celebrity idol. When some actress has gained such cultural clout and evokes such emulation as to be able to set fashion in hair styles, clothes, and behavior, she is said to be a matinee idol. When four wrestlers in Iran committed suicide, the Associated Press said it was because their "idol had killed himself." A large number of poison-pen letters in England were sent to the parents of a four-year-old who had been savagely mauled by an Alsatian guard dog. The dog had subsequently been killed and the writers blamed the child's parents. Reuter's wire service added: "The letters have come from all over Britain, traditionally a dog-worshipping country." A similar response occurred in some quarters when there was more criticism of Russia for orbiting a dog into space than for her brutal suppression of people in the Hungarian revolt. Today's popular media sees such veneration of animals as a reflection of the ancient and biblical understanding of worship as extreme veneration. It is in contrast to the narrow ecclesiastical definitions that insist that worship always means God.

One of Karl Marx's keenest insights was that man's work tends to mold him in the image of his task. As man serves (*therapeuo*) his task he is shaped by it. When one moves to another city the children are not asked who their father is but what he does. His identity is shaped by his task. A tombstone in England reads: ". . . born a man, died a green grocer." "I am a housewife" is not enough identity, nor is any job.

Man's grandeur is that he can worship nothing in this world that will not diminish him for he is made in the image of God. Man's misery is that he perversely continues to fashion things to create his own image. Hence it is not a matter of whether we worship but what we worship. Friedman is an excellent guide in discerning some of the very sinister but unnoticed models or images that are diminishing modern man. But his brave alternative, the qualified mosaic of the seven figures fashioned by the mind of existential authors, though a better idol than most, is an idol nevertheless. There is something sadly stoic and Promethean in the final hope: "The readiness to meet what is essentially other and hold one's ground when one meets it, the Dialogue with the Absurd in which trust and contending are inseparably conjoined."

The fundamental corollary of worship and such image-making is that one becomes like what he worships; we emulate what we venerate, serve, open ourselves to, esteem, and affirm.

HUBRIS AND MODERN IDOLATRY

In both pagan and Christian experience man's confidence in resolving for himself his own identity has been called *hubris*: "the personification of overweening pride in which man, heedless of his mortal nature and losing all sense of measure, allows his skill, his power, and his good fortune to make him arrogant towards god; Nemesis." Allen Wheelis, in *The Quest for Identity* speaks for many secular men: "Modern man cannot recapture an identity out of the past; for his old identity was not lost, but outgrown. Identity is not, therefore, to be found; it is to be created and achieved." The tragic result of such arrogance is that the identity which man is creating and achieving is in the process of eroding what humanity he does have. Paul Tillich's term for such confidence of self-creation is "autonomy," whereby man is a law unto himself.

Jean Paul Sartre recognizes that without God it is not an option but absolutely necessary that man rely on his own *hubris.*

> If I've discarded God the father, there has to be someone to invent values. . . . To say that we invent values means nothing else but this: life has no meaning *a priori.* Before you come alive, life is nothing; it's up to you to give it a meaning, and value is nothing else but the meaning that you choose.

There is something quite refreshing in the clear candor with which Sartre sees the necessary results of discarding the Father. He tells us that he "grew like a weed on the compost of Catholicity; my roots sucked up its juices and I changed them into sap." But also he rather poignantly states: "I was taught Sacred History, the Gospel, and the catechism without being given the means for believing." Yet in the play, *No Exit,* Sartre can disclose the human condition without God's grace in a far more biblical way than most Christian attempts. Man is left in the play, however, with the necessity of not only creating his own values and identity but of being his own god.

In contrast to this spirit the greatest artists have always groped for some way to express their sense that, whatever creativity they had, it came to them from some source other than themselves. Humility, in the face of their own work, has been symbolized since pagan times by the word *muse.* The true source of inspiration and creativity is not considered a possession. It comes to the artist in the most frustrating, unpredictable, and unscheduled way. Sometimes it comes not at all. Most of us, who stand in awe of great creative talent such as Tennessee Williams, are surprised to discover his abject fear at the end of each accomplishment of having nothing else to say. As it is often put: "It will not be given to him to create so well again." It could well be that such humility in the face of man's limitations is actually the occasion of an artist's openness and expectancy without which there would be no power to create.

Nothing seems to express this humility better than the passive voice used to describe man's being an agent in a creative act. The active voice means one acts, while the passive voice means that one is acted upon. Albert Einstein used to walk to work at Princeton with Robert Oppenheimer and the latter tells of Einstein once breaking the usual silence with the observation: "When it has been once given to you to do something rather reasonable, forever afterwards your work and life are a little strange." This passive voice, ". . . when it has once been given," has been used by extraordinarily creative persons since pagan times in exploring the source or genesis of their creativity. But the tide of modern times is going in the opposite direction, as Philip Rieff points out:

What men lose when they become as free as gods is precisely that sense of being chosen, which encourages them, in their gratitude, to take their subsequent choices seriously. Put in another way, this means: Freedom does not exist without responsibility.

The *National Geographic* (October, 1969) had a most interesting article about Charles Darwin by Alan Villiers, who had retraced the voyage of the "Beagle" around the world and photographed the places where Darwin had stopped a hundred years ago. In his narrative Villiers introduces a number of quotations from Darwin's diary. What strikes the reader is the difference in perspective between Darwin and Villiers. The former speaks of the ocean that "was here spread out," one species of bird "had been taken and modified for different ends," searching for the grand scheme "on which organized beings have been created," a special variety "had been modified for different ends." Villiers, a faithful representative of our age with its characteristic *hubris,* infers from Darwin's findings that all change, modification, and design is from within creation, autogenous, autonomous. He writes: "No wonder the local cormorant *has evolved* into a flightless bird. . . ." (italics mine.)

WORSHIP AND FINDING OURSELVES

Christian worship, as against all forms of idolatry, is always and primarily rendered in the passive voice, in the expectancy and primacy of God's action and Word. In such worship we do not invent values but discern them. We do not fashion our own identities but we are shaped and refashioned by the Spirit of God. Abraham, Moses, the prophets, and the disciples were all called. God's word came to them and their work was a response.

"God is a Spirit: and they that worship him must worship him in spirit and in truth." (John 4:24) As we have seen in the last chapter, we see with our wills and hear with our hearts; so also we worship with our wills and hearts. Since we cannot will to change our wills and cannot hear without the Word, we can neither see nor hear until the story is told. "In the beginning was the Word. . . ." That was the Word God spoke. It was no letter, law, nor ideal but Jesus who can only be discerned as Christ by the inner man. He himself is the food for the will and the heart, "Feed on him in thy heart by faith with thanksgiving."

The fundamental theme in the Bible, as well as in this book, is righteousness. He is the "God of my righteousness" (Ps. 4:1). Righteousness is the "habitation of his throne" (Ps. 97:2). God's "righteousness endureth forever" (Ps. 112:3,9). God's name is "the Lord our righteousness" (Jer. 23:6). "Blessed are those who hunger and thirst after righteousness" (Matt. 5:6). We wait "for the hope of righteousness" (Gal. 5:5). We are they "to whom God imputeth (words, treats as, regards as) righteousness without works" (Rom. 4:6). "For the promise . . . was not . . . through the law (civilization) but through the righteousness of faith (the self's center)" (Rom. 4:13). ". . . Not having mine own righteousness . . . but the righteousness which is of God by faith" (Phil. 3:9).

We have already shown in Chapter 3 that God's good word to our root problem of disesteem/self-hatred is the word of forgiveness that removes, takes away, eradicates the threat of rejection and condemnation. This forgiveness of God is not a winking at wickedness, but the means by which he begins to make the wicked right.

The crucial issue of guilt is resolved on this foundation of God's acceptance and initiates the movement toward our health and wholeness (salvation). Our true guilt is the shadow we cast as we walk in God's light. It outlines, indicates, and adumbrates the righteousness we serve and will be like.

Destructive anger, generated by the pressure of law and aggravated by civilization, is sucked up and buried by the pain, passion, and death of the only one who was ever fully right. We who are wrong are begun to be made right by being held accountable and responsible (able to respond) to the love that took and takes our anger.

The threat of death is overcome by the resurrection, the "righteousness on God's terms," that bars, flunks, expels, and destroys sin. The only thing we need fear to lose in the resurrection is our own sin.

The means by which we see, hear, and know what is truly right are the same means by which we grow, are fed, and nurtured in the inner man—our wills and our hearts. Our identity is fashioned by the veneration, service, esteem, and openness to this righteousness we see in Christ. The Word that is not bread alone is always Jesus Christ. He is portrayed anew by Langmead Casserley.

His was a real babyhood and youth, a real growth in mind and stature, a desperately human hunger, an exquisitely human pain, an agonizingly human death. In His thirty years of incarnate existence, God was touched and harrowed by all that is most menacing in the lot of man—physical pain, economic insecurity, subtle temptation, a tragic death foreseen and awaited, the frustration of noble purposes, intellectual misunderstanding, the wearisome, disillusioning absence of sympathy, slander, unpopularity, injustice, persecution, rejected love. All that most easily overcomes the spirit of man He faced without defeat, all that is most prone to embitter and distort the human character He absorbed without bitterness or spiritual loss, smiled kindly through the endless frustrations which so often cynicize and disillusion romantic and idealistic men, loved unwearingly through the rejection of love with a love which not even hatred could remould in its own image, confronted temptation with an invincible perfection of character and purpose against which the hitherto victorious powers of evil were powerless, and finally placed in the hands of death a life so intense and concentrated on its destiny that death's age-old mastery over life was revealed as a broken thing.

There is a well known episode in the Book of Joshua in which he challenges his people to choose "this day whom you will serve."

For Christians this Lord is Jesus Christ:

through whom God declared his righteousness in forgiving sinners,
whose love is the goal toward which our true guilt is tugging us,
who took and takes our anger on himself,
who is the sure and certain hope of resurrection and the triumph of final rightness,
who is the image of our health and humanity,
whom we know by the knowledge of the heart,
whom we see by the service of our wills.

"And if it seem evil unto you to serve the Lord, choose you this day whom you will serve . . . but as for me and my house, we will serve the Lord." (Joshua 24:15)

AUTHOR'S NOTES

THE READER will find listed here by chapter bibliographical information only on those authors and books from which quotation has been made. They appear in the order of their citation in the text. In a few special instances information is also included on background titles of special importance.

Chapter One
FOUR CONTEMPORARY PATTERNS

Sigmund Freud, *Civilization and Its Discontents* (London: Hogarth Press, 1957), p. 123; see also 136–142 for his use of word "civilization" as synonymous with cultural superego.
Mary Chase, *Harvey*. By permission of Brandt and Brandt.

Chapter Two
MODELS FOR THEIR RESOLUTION

Norman O. Brown, *Love's Body* (New York: Random House, 1966), p. 266.
Theodore Roszak, *The Making of a Counter Culture* (New York: Doubleday, 1968), p. 116.
Philip Rieff, *The Triumph of the Therapeutic* (New York: Harper and Row, 1965), p. 234.
Freud, *Civilization and Its Discontents*, pp. 143–144.

Chapter Three
SELF-ESTEEM RESTORED

Roy Lee, *Freud and Christianity* (London: James Clarke, 1949). See pp. 79, 80, 194, 195.

Jeremy Taylor, The Whole Works of the Rt. Rev. Jeremy Taylor (London: Reginald Heber, 1828), VI, 258; 259; 587; 64.

Freud, *Civilization and Its Discontents*, pp. 139–140.

G. and F. Kittel, eds., *Theological Dictionary of the New Testament* (Grand Rapids: Eerdmans), IV, 284–289. See *logidzomai*; my discussion is based on this entry.

Chapter Four
GUILT REDEEMED

Edward Stein, *Guilt: Theory and Therapy* (Philadelphia: Westminster, 1968), pp. 14; 23; 13.

Theodore Reik, *Myth and Guilt*. See pp. 330 ff. on destructive ethic.

J. D. Unwin, *Sex and Culture* (London: Oxford University Press, 1934), p. 412.

Chapter Five
ANGER ATONED

Anthony Storr, *Human Aggression* (New York: Atheneum, 1969). See Chapter 1 and pp. 113–115, for a discussion of the question of instinctual factors in human aggression. The first quotation is from p. 2; the second from p. 115.

Archibald MacLeish, *J. B.* (Boston: Houghton Mifflin, 1958), pp. 11; 14; 99; and 90.

Johann Heerman (1630) in *The Hymnal, 1940* (New York: The Church Pension Fund), Hymn 71.

Walter Russell Bowie, Hymn 522, in *The Hymnal, 1940*.

Chapter Six
THE LAST ENEMY OVERCOME

The interview with Eugene Ionesco by Rosette Lamont appeared in *Horizon,* May, 1961.

Rollo May, *Love and Will* (New York: W. W. Norton, 1969), p. 106.

Norman O. Brown, *Life Against Death* (London: Routledge and Kegan Paul, 1959), p. 104.

Donald Rogan, *Campus Apocalypse* (New York: Seabury Press, 1969), pp. 143–145.

Milton Gatch, *Death* (New York: Seabury Press, 1969), p. 163.

Nathan A. Scott, ed., *The Modern Vision of Death* (Richmond: John Knox Press, 1967), pp. 70–71 for the Morganthau quotation (italics are mine). By permission.

Archibald MacLeish, *J. B.* (Boston: Houghton Mifflin, 1958), p. 151.

W. H. Auden, *The Collected Poetry of W. H. Auden* (New York: Random House, 1945), p. 411 for the poem "For the Time Being."

Scott, ed., *The Modern Vision of Death*. The Wilder quotations, pp. 19; 26. The Morganthau quotation, pp. 70–71.

Taylor, *The Whole Works,* p. 302.

Chapter Seven
KNOWING GOD IN THE AGE OF HIS "DEATH"

W. Hooper, ed., *Selected Literary Essays* (Cambridge University Press, 1969), for C. S. Lewis' essay *"De Descriptione Temporum."*

J. Hillis Miller, *The Disappearance of God* (New York: Schocken Books, 1965), p. 359.

Kenneth Clark, *Civilization* (New York: Harper and Row, 1970), p. 185.

W. B. Yeats, *The Collected Poems of W. B. Yeats* (New York: Macmillan, 1956), pp. 211; 230–231.

Erich Fromm, *Psychoanalysis and Religion* (New Haven: Yale University Press, 1950), p. 126.

Rieff, *The Triumph of the Therapeutic*, pp. 251–252; 4.

Allen Wheelis, *The Quest for Identity* (New York: W. W. Norton and Company, 1958), pp. 209–210 (italics mine).

May, *Love and Will*, p. 25.

Theodore Roszak, *The Making of a Counter Culture* (New York: Doubleday, 1969), pp. 98; 12. See also p. 120; and especially pp. 231–233.

Michael Polanyi, *Personal Knowledge*: Towards a Post-Critical Philosophy (Chicago University Press, 1959).

N. Kazantzakis, *The Last Temptation of Christ* (New York: Simon and Schuster), p. 196.

Bertrand Russell, *The Scientific Outlook* (New York: W. W. Norton, 1931), pp. 262; and also 263f.

Nelvin Vos, "Eugene Ionesco, Edward Albee" (Grand Rapids: Eerdmans, 1968).

William Derham, *The Christian Philosopher* (London, 1721), p. 166.

Sigmund Freud, *The Future of an Illusion* (London: Hogarth Press, 1927), p. 57.

Lee, *Freud and Christianity*, p. 18.

Stein, *Guilt: Theory and Therapy*, p. 194–195.

Hugh Trevor-Roper, *Men and Events* (New York: St. Martin's Press, 1957).

William Porcher DuBose, *The Ecumenical Councils* (New York: The Christian Literature Co.), pp. 52–53.

Chapter Eight
FINDING IDENTITY IN WORSHIP

Erik H. Erikson, *Identity: Youth and Crisis* (New York: W. W. Norton, 1968), pp. 18–19.

Julian Hartt, *The Lost Image of Man* (Baton Rouge: The Louisiana State University Press, 1963), for an excellent discussion on the identity question.

Stephen F. Bayne, "Make Room for Man." Address, October 29, 1943, Columbia University.

Roszak, *The Making of a Counter Culture.*

Maurice Friedman, *The Problematic Rebel* (New York: Random House, 1963). See also *To Deny Our Nothingness* (New York: Delacorte Press, 1967); quotation, p. 372.

Auden, *Collected Works,* p. 426.

Evelyn Underhill, *Worship* (New York: Harper, 1936), pp. 3 and 6.

Jean-Paul Sartre, *Existentialism* (New York: Philosophical Library, 1947), p. 58. See also *Words* (Greenwich: Fawcett, 1964), pp. 156, 157.

Rieff, *The Triumph of the Therapeutic,* p. 93.

Nathan Scott, *The Broken Center* (New Haven: Yale University Press, 1966), p. 113.